TOUGH QUESTIONS JEWS ASK

A Young Adult's Guide to Building a Jewish Life

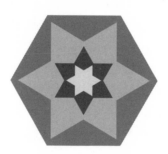

RABBI EDWARD FEINSTEIN

JEWISH LIGHTS Publishing
Woodstock, Vermont

Tough Questions Jews Ask:
A Young Adult's Guide to Building a Jewish Life

2005 Third printing
2003 Second printing
2003 First printing
© 2003 by Edward Feinstein

For information regarding permission to reprint material from this book, please write or fax your request to Jewish Lights Publishing, Permissions Department, at the address / fax number listed below, or e-mail your request to permissions@jewishlights.com.

Library of Congress Cataloging-in-Publication Data
Feinstein, Edward, 1964–
Tough questions Jews ask : a young adult's guide to building a Jewish life / Edward Feinstein.
    p. cm.
ISBN 1-58023-139-X (pbk.)
1. Jewish way of life. 2. Judaism—Customs and practices. I. Title.
BM723 .F43 2003
296.7'0835—dc21

                                                                2002154425

10 9 8 7 6 5 4 3

Manufactured in the United States of America

Cover Design: Bronwen Battaglia

Published by Jewish Lights Publishing
A Division of LongHill Partners, Inc.
Sunset Farm Offices, Route 4, P.O. Box 237
Woodstock, VT 05091
Tel: (802) 457-4000 Fax: (802) 457-4004
www.jewishlights.com

Contents

 *How to Read This Book*

I've always had lots of questions—tough questions, the kind of questions that just won't go away. Even though I had wonderful teachers growing up, teachers who listened patiently and tried to help me find answers, my list of questions just kept growing. (Good questions never go away.) One of the reasons I started studying to be a rabbi was to find answers to my own questions.

When I became a rabbi, I promised myself that I would never turn away anyone who had a good question. And so, for more than twenty years I've been listening to questions—from kids and adults, from teens and seniors, from Christians and Jews. Some questions have easy answers. Most of the really good questions can't be answered at all. I've tried to help people think about their questions and seek out their own answers.

This book is a collection of some of the best questions

I've been asked and the responses that have helped people think more deeply. To make it fun, I imagined that the people who asked the best questions were all in one class. So the class I describe here is made up, but the questions are real and the people who asked are real. (I changed their names to keep their parents from getting mad at them for giving the rabbi a hard time!)

You can read the chapters in order, or you can skip around. You might want to keep a log of your own answers to the questions and a list of new questions that come up as you're reading.

As you read this book, please remember that there are many, many different ways to be Jewish. There are many different ways to understand and practice the Jewish religion. There are many ways to come close to God. There are many ways to answer life's toughest questions. We Jews are like a family sharing conversation at the dinner table. There is never only one right opinion, never only one way to be Jewish. These answers are one person's ideas and interpretations. I'm a rabbi, and I've spent a great deal of time thinking and learning about these things, but I'm still just one person. You can agree or disagree with me; you can argue with me. (In fact, I hope you will.) Your parents, your teachers, even other rabbis may have completely different answers to the questions. I hope you'll go and ask them to share their ideas. Most of all, I hope you will never stop asking. I believe that God loves good questions.

 *Acknowledgments*

I am grateful to all those who have asked me tough questions over the years, including the kids, staff, and families of the Solomon Schechter Academy of Dallas, where I was principal; Congregation Shearith Israel, where I was rabbi; Camp Ramah in California, where I was the director; the Ziegler Rabbinical School of the University of Judaism, where I teach; and Valley Beth Shalom, where I'm a rabbi.

I have been very fortunate over the years to have many loving teachers who listened to my endless questions. These include Rabbi Elijah J. Schochet, Professor Elliot N. Dorff, Professor Neil Gillman, Rabbi David Hartman, and my mentor, Rabbi Harold M. Schulweis. I've been blessed with loving colleagues and friends who have helped me seek the answers. I am grateful to every one of them for sharing their wisdom and support.

I thank my editor, Bryna Fischer, for her help and patience. I thank Stuart M. Matlins, publisher, and the people at Jewish Lights for making this book and so many works of light and wisdom accessible to thinking, seeking souls.

And I thank God for the blessing of a loving family; for my parents, Dov and Chaiky, Herb and Geri; for our kids, Yonah, Nessa, and Raffi; and for Nina, who has answered so many of my questions.

Am I Allowed to Ask?

DOES IT MAKE GOD MAD
IF WE ASK QUESTIONS?

They were the worst class anyone could remember. "Teacher-slayers," they were called. It was only December and already they had sent three teachers into early retirement. Mrs. Goldenberg, a veteran of years of teaching seventh grade, left after a month of their rude behavior and cruel practical jokes. Mr. Weinberg presented himself as a "cool" young teacher who rode a motorcycle to the synagogue and quoted lyrics from the latest songs. He lasted a week and a half. Ms. Alon, once a sergeant in the Israeli army, had survived real terrorists, but she couldn't survive this class.

I was the last resort. I'm the rabbi. I'm supposed to know how to perform miracles.

I suppose it was something of a miracle that happened. The kids in the class realized that it was one thing to knock off a few ordinary teachers; it was quite another thing to get on the wrong side of your rabbi. After all, they all looked forward to celebrating a Bar or Bat Mitzvah in the coming year. And for that, you need the rabbi.

When I walked into the room, they were ready. Not with their usual greeting of foul words, bored looks, spitballs, and paper airplanes, but with a sort of petition.

Dear Rabbi,

As you know, this is our graduating year in the Hebrew School. But we still have lots of questions that never got answered in the years we've been here. Instead of learning the stuff in the book, could we please spend the time we have left this year answering these questions?

Respectfully,

The Seventh Grade Class

"Sounds like a great idea," I responded. "Let's begin right away. I'll try to answer any questions you have. What's your first one?"

There was a moment of silence, as if they hadn't really expected me to go along with the idea. And then the girl who handed me the petition said softly, "I have lots of questions about God and stuff, but I'm afraid if I tell you, you won't let me have my Bat Mitzvah. So I wonder, are we really allowed to ask you questions? Does it make God mad if we ask questions?"

That's how we started.

Let me tell you about my Bar Mitzvah. The week before my Bar Mitzvah, I was a mess. I had just turned thirteen. I was becoming an adult, or so everyone was telling me. I was scheduled to stand up in front of the rabbi, my family, and the congregation and tell everyone how proud I was to be Jewish. But I was so full of questions! W*hy* am I Jewish? Do I really believe in all this? Do I really believe in God? Do I believe the stories in the Torah or the words of the prayer book? How can I believe God exists if the world is so full of suffering? Who needs a Bar Mitzvah, anyway? How can I honestly go through with a Bar Mitzvah if I'm so full of questions?

I had an uncle who was an important rabbi. He spent a lifetime learning and teaching Torah at an Orthodox college in Chicago. Just before my Bar Mitzvah, he moved to Los Angeles, where we lived. My father thought it would be a good idea for me to meet Uncle Mottel. So Dad drove me to Uncle Mottel's apartment, introduced me, then disappeared.

I sat, trembling, in front of my uncle. He asked me about my studies and how I'd prepared for my Bar Mitzvah. I told him what I'd learned. And then from somewhere deep in me came something I hadn't meant to say, "Uncle Mottel, do you ever have questions that just won't go away? Do you ever wonder if God is real? Do you ever wonder if the Torah is true? Do you ever wonder why you're Jewish?"

For a moment, I was embarrassed and scared.

Maybe he'd get mad and throw me out! Maybe he'd recite some ancient curse and turn me into a worm! Maybe he'd cancel my Bar Mitzvah and expel me from the Jewish people. But Uncle Mottel smiled kindly and answered softly, "Do I have questions? Do I wonder about God? Every single day! Every day I wonder if God is real, if the Torah is true. Every day I wonder why I'm a Jew. But that's part of being Jewish. In the Torah, we're called Yisrael—the ones who wrestle with God. Wrestling, asking, wondering, searching is just what God wants us to do! God loves good questions! Now tell me, what are your questions?" He listened with patience and concentration.

We spent two hours and a whole six-pack of soda talking through my questions and his questions, his answers and my answers. Every question brought an answer. And every answer brought a new question. He pulled down dozens of old books filled with wisdom—the Bible, volumes of the Talmud, and books of Hasidic stories. "Study these books," he instructed me. "You will find many others who asked your questions. Study these books and join their discussion! That's what it means to be Yisrael, to be a Jew."

A week later, I stood on the *bimah* of the synagogue for my Bar Mitzvah. I was nervous. After all, every kid from my class was there! But I wasn't worried about my questions any longer. Uncle Mottel had invited me to wonder, to ask questions, to join the discussion of those who have spent more than three thousand years wondering and asking— the Jewish people, my people.

In Judaism, you're allowed to ask questions. You're invited to ask questions. In fact, asking questions is about the most important thing Jewish people do. In the Bible, Abraham, the first Jew, asks God a zinger of a question: "How can You, the Judge of all the earth, not do what's right?" (Genesis 18:25). The most important moment in the Passover seder is the asking of a question: "Why is tonight different from all other nights?" The Talmud, the great encyclopedia of Jewish wisdom, teaches that if you're too embarrassed to ask questions, you'll never learn anything (*Pirke Avot* 2:5).

Why are questions so important? Because we're Jewish with our entire self—our thoughts, our feelings, and our actions. We're not allowed to leave out any part of ourselves. The Torah teaches, "You will love the Lord your God with all your heart, with all your life, and with all your strength" (Deuteronomy 6:5). Notice the word "all." Your whole self must be involved. You're not allowed to believe in something that makes no sense to you. You're not allowed to do things that feel wrong to you. Thinking, feeling, believing, and doing must be whole. People get into trouble when they feel without thinking, believe without thinking, or do without thinking. If it doesn't make sense—ask! If it doesn't feel right—ask! As a Jew, that's what is expected of you!

2

Who Believes in God Anymore?

WHY SHOULD I BELIEVE IN GOD? WHY SHOULD ANYONE?

Billy was acknowledged by everyone to be the smartest kid in the class. For fun, he tore apart computers and put them together again. He spent most of his Hebrew School hours reading science fiction. But with the rabbi in the room, he saw a chance to set a few things straight.

"Rabbi, I believe in science. I believe in evolution. I believe in nature. But I don't believe in God. Why should I believe in God? Why should anyone?"

A rabbi I know once asked a class of teenagers, "How many of you believe in God?" Not one hand went up.

"Rabbi, no one believes in God anymore!" they explained.

The rabbi was heartbroken. These were great kids. They were involved in the life of his synagogue. "How could they not believe in God?" he wondered. So he spent the rest of the class trying to convince them. He showed them all sorts of impressive philosophical proofs and arguments. But at the end of the class, the kids said to him, "Nice try, Rabbi. But we still don't believe in God."

The rabbi went home that night with a terrible headache. This class really depressed him. He met with the class again the following week. This time, he asked a different question: "When in your life did you ever feel that God was close to you?"

Every kid in the class had an answer.

One boy said, "Every Friday night, my mom lights candles for Shabbat. She says a quiet prayer and her eyes get filled up with tears. And somehow I know that God is listening to her prayers."

Another student said, "When my grandfather died, the whole family came to the cemetery. We all stood around his grave and told stories of his life. Somehow, I knew that God was close then."

A girl said, "Last summer, my family took a trip to Israel. At the same time that our plane landed, a plane of Jews from Russia or someplace also landed. Those people were so glad to get to Israel that they got down on their knees and kissed the ground. At that moment, I knew that God was close."

Have you ever felt that God was close to you? I think

that at some time or another, almost everyone has had a feeling that God is close. These are often the most powerful moments in our lives. These are the moments that let us know that our lives are very special. We may not know what God is. We may not have words to describe God. But we have a strong sense that God is close.

Several years ago, I was diagnosed with cancer. My doctors told me that I might not have long to live. An emergency operation was followed by months of very unpleasant medicine. This was the most terrifying time in my life. I started to wonder if there was a God who cared for me. And then I met Charles. Charles was a night nurse in the hospital. He and I came from different worlds: I'm a Jew from California; he's an African-American Baptist from Alabama. But each night, Charles came to my hospital room to care for me. When I complained, which I did a lot, he told me jokes. When I was in pain, he made me feel better. When I didn't want to take my medicine, he yelled at me. When I was scared, he gave me strength and inspiration. Each morning, he came one last time to check on me and leave me with a thought for the day. "You have faith now, Rabbi!" he would say. No amount of money in the world could pay Charles for what he did for me. And as I fought this cancer, I discovered that the world is filled with people like Charles. This is what the Bible means when it says that people are "created in God's image" (Genesis 1:27). Through their kindness, we can feel God close by.

Believing in God is not a matter of accepting an abstract idea. Believing in God means gathering in the moments when God feels close by and taking these moments seriously. It means remembering these moments, cherishing them, and saving them. It means pursuing them. And it means learning from them.

How do we find such important moments? If we want a moment with Mom or Dad, we know how to find them. If we want a moment with a teacher, we might go up after class. How do we get a moment with God?

Over the generations of Jewish history, many Jews have had moments when they felt God was close. Because these moments were so important, they wanted to share them with us. So they left behind a trail for us to follow. The trail is marked by a special line of words you might already know:

בָּרוּךְ אַתָּה יְיָ אֱלֹהֵינוּ מֶלֶךְ הָעוֹלָם.

Baruch Ata Adonai, Elohaynu melech ha-olam.
Praised are You, God, Ruler of the Universe.

What we call a *"bracha"*—a blessing—is more than a prayer. It is a trail marker showing us the way to find a moment with God. What comes next in the *bracha* is most important— the description of a moment with God. For example:

בָּרוּךְ אַתָּה יְיָ אֱלֹהֵינוּ מֶלֶךְ הָעוֹלָם
הַמּוֹצִיא לֶחֶם מִן הָאָרֶץ.

Baruch Ata Adonai, Elohaynu melech ha-olam,
ha-motzee lechem min ha-aretz.

Praised are You, God, Ruler of the Universe,
who brings bread from the earth.

Even something regular and boring, like eating my sandwich for lunch, can become a moment when I can feel God is close.

Feeding the world, this *bracha* tells us, is something God does. But it is also something we can do. We can grow food. We can prepare a meal. We can feed hungry people. And when we do that, we are sharing with God the work of feeding people, and we feel God is close.

Near our synagogue, there is a shelter for homeless families. Several times a year, kids from our synagogue youth group go there to prepare and serve meals. I once asked the kids what it feels like to share a meal with people who have nothing and who have known only hunger and want. One kid answered, "I held a serving spoon, and God held my hand."

How do we find moments with God like that one? We look at the *brachot*, the blessings, and follow the path:

בָּרוּךְ אַתָּה יְיָ אֱלֹהֵינוּ מֶלֶךְ הָעוֹלָם
פּוֹקֵחַ עִוְרִים;
מַלְבִּישׁ עֲרוּמִים;
מַתִּיר אֲסוּרִים.

Baruch Ata Adonai, Elohaynu melech ha-olam,

pokeach eev'reem;

malbeesh arumeem;

mateer asureem.

Praised are You, God, Ruler of the Universe,

who helps the blind see;

who gives clothing to the naked;

who frees those who are confined.

These are moments with God that are waiting for you. Could you do any of these things?

I believe that God is real. But God isn't far off in heaven; God is right here. How do we know God is near? By feeling the caring presence of others, of people like Charles. And by feeling our own power to care and to help. We can be God's hands, God's eyes, and God's ears in the world. We can bring God close to others when they are in need, just as others bring God close to us.

Ultimately, the bigger question isn't, "Should I believe in God?" but rather, "What difference does it make?" What difference does it make if there is God? I don't think the point is just to say that God exists, and then go on living as before. The point is to be like God, to live a Godly life. The point is to be a person like Charles and do the caring that God needs done in the world. Because when we care, God is real and close.

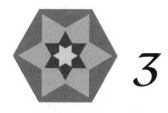

3

Do I Have to Go to Services? What Good Is Praying?

DOES GOD LISTEN? DOES GOD ANSWER?

"I have to go to services on Saturday for my friend's Bar Mitzvah," reported Daniel to the class. "I hate services. They're sooooo boring." Daniel was being honest. Then, he suddenly remembered that I'm the rabbi, so he retreated. "You go to services every Saturday. Don't you find it boring?"

"No, actually, I like praying," I told him.

This, he couldn't believe. "You actually like it? Why? What good is praying? Does God listen? Does God answer you?"

Abraham Joshua Heschel was an important rabbi and philosopher who lived in the middle of the twentieth century. Heschel traveled around the world, teaching in synagogues, churches, and universities. Whenever he gave an evening lecture, he would begin by telling the audience, "Ladies and gentlemen, a great miracle just happened!" People would stop to listen very carefully, wondering: What miracle happened? Why didn't we see it? Then Heschel would continue, "A great miracle just happened: The sun went down!" Some people would laugh. Some would shake their heads at this crazy rabbi. Others remained puzzled about what he meant. Then Heschel would begin to talk about how a religious person sees the world.

Miracles happen all the time, Heschel taught. Amazing things, magnificent things are happening all around us. But most of us don't notice. We have learned how to ignore them.

We normally think that miracles are events that break the laws of nature—seas that split, plagues that fall from the sky, or sticks that turn into snakes. Heschel understood that the most remarkable things are not these rare and unusual events, but the normal, regular, everyday things that we never notice. How can normal things be miracles? It's all in how we look at them.

Have you ever been really sick? Do you remember how wonderful it felt when you started to get better? Do you remember when the fever went away, or the first time that you could swallow without pain? It's an amazing feeling. Maybe you promised yourself that you'd never forget how great it feels. You promised that you'd appreciate your health and never take being healthy for granted again! That lasted about thirty minutes, and then you forgot; we all do.

What could be more wonderful than being healthy—feeling all the parts of your body working well? Being healthy is a miracle, but one that most of us never notice. Yet how much happier would we be if we could just notice each day how wonderful it is to be healthy? We would probably complain a lot less about small things that bother and annoy us if we looked upon our health as a precious gift. And we might take better care of ourselves.

The religious person, taught Heschel, notices the miracles. The religious person notices how amazing things—all things—really are. The religious person stops and wonders at the beauty of a sunset, the power of a thunderstorm, and the kindness of a stranger. The opposite of being religious, according to Heschel, isn't a person who doesn't believe in God, but a person who doesn't notice all the amazing things around us. The opposite of being religious is being bored.

We've discussed the moments we have when we feel God close to us. Heschel believed that these moments can happen all the time. The problem is that we're distracted. We're too busy. We have homework to complete and piano to practice. We have TV shows to watch and phone calls to make. We have places to go and things to do. We are very busy people. And we miss the opportunities to feel God close by.

Prayer is a way to learn how to stop and notice the miracles around us. Prayer is a way to have a moment with God. Most people think that prayer is a way of asking for things from God, but only a very little bit of Jewish prayer is "asking prayer." Most Jewish prayers get us to stop and notice. Prayer in Judaism is a way to learn mindfulness—how to pay attention to the miracles that are all around us.

How do you wake up in the morning? I'm not what you'd call a "morning person." I wake up with a grumble and a groan. I'm usually late, so there's a rush to the bathroom, to breakfast, and then out the door to work. Never do I notice the miracle of a new day—a new chance at living, a new chance at learning, a new chance to find friendship. So I've learned to force myself to stop for just a few seconds and say a prayer:

מוֹדֶה אֲנִי לְפָנֶיךָ, מֶלֶךְ חַי וְקַיָּם,
שֶׁהֶחֱזַרְתָּ בִּי נִשְׁמָתִי בְּחֶמְלָה; רַבָּה אֱמוּנָתֶךָ.

Modeh ani lefanecha melech chai v'kayam sheh-hech-
ezar-ta bee nishmatee bichemla raba emoonatecha.
Thank you God, Source of Life, for the gifts of
life and energy and this new day.

Take ten seconds each morning to stop and say thank you for the miracle of this new day. Take ten seconds to think about what's possible in this new day and what you could do with this day.

The purpose of prayer is not to change God. The purpose of prayer is to change us. The purpose of prayer is to make us aware of the miracles around us and the moments of God's closeness waiting for us each day. Prayer doesn't bring heaven down; prayer brings us up. So the question in the end is not, Does God hear my prayers? Rather, ask: Do I hear my prayers? Am I listening? Am I paying attention? Do I notice the miracles happening around me all the time?

Class discussion

IF I PRAY FOR SOMETHING, WILL I GET IT?

Daniel wasn't satisfied.

"On Hanukkah, I asked God for a certain toy. I didn't get it. Did God forget about me? If I pray for something, will I get it? Does God answer that kind of prayer?"

Suppose you have test in a class you don't like, so you don't bother to study. (You'd rather watch TV.) A few minutes before the test, you begin praying, "Please God, help me on this test!" Will it help? Three days later, the teacher passes back your test. She puts the paper face down on your desk. You're scared to look at the grade. So, you pray again, "Please God, let it be a good grade!" Will it help?

In the Talmud, there's an important teaching:

A woman is pregnant and about to give birth. Her husband wants a son, so he prays, "Please God, let it be a boy!" This is an empty prayer. A man coming home from a trip hears a fire alarm in his town. He prays, "Please God, not my house!" This is empty prayer (*Brachot* 54a).

Jewish tradition believes in the power of prayer—but only intelligent prayer. There are intelligent prayers, and there are empty prayers. Why are these prayers empty?

The father who prays for a son is asking God to change something that's already been determined. God doesn't work that way. That's an empty prayer.

The person who prays that the emergency be at someone else's house is asking God to change something that's already been determined—and more, he's asking that something bad be put on someone else. That's *really* empty prayer.

There is a difference between prayer and magic. A magician pretends to use his powers to change things in the world just by saying magic words. The most famous magic words are actually an old Hebrew spell: A*bra-Kadabra* is Hebrew for "I will make it as I say it."

We know that magic is not real. Rabbits don't come out of hats. And the lady isn't really cut in two and then re-attached. It's pretend.

Expecting God to change the world just because you want it changed is also magic. And like magic, it's not real. It doesn't happen. God doesn't work that way. That's empty prayer.

So you didn't study for the test and you got a bad grade. But this issue of empty prayer can be much more serious: A mom and dad once came to talk with me. They were very upset because their daughter had been diagnosed with a terrible disease. They prayed and prayed, but the daughter's condition only got worse. They asked me, "Why doesn't God answer our prayers and make her better?" They figured that God must have some reason to ignore their prayers, and that reason must have something to do with them. They imagined that they had done something wrong and that God was punishing them. "What did we do to deserve this? Why is God so mad at us?" they asked me through their tears.

I felt so badly for these people—they were really hurting. First, they hurt because their child was sick. Second, they hurt more by believing that God refused to hear their prayers because of something they had done. They ended up believing that they had brought pain on their child, which is the worst pain a parent can feel. Third, they hurt even more because they couldn't figure out what they had done that was so bad to deserve such a punishment and what they could do about it. Sometimes even just an idea can really hurt.

Real prayer, prayer that works, I explained to them, doesn't change the world; it changes us. We can't ask God to change the world for us. We have to do that for ourselves. We can only ask God for the wisdom, strength, and courage to change it ourselves. When I was sick with cancer, I told them, I didn't pray for the cancer to go away. I knew that was an empty prayer. I prayed, instead, for the courage to keep hoping and not give up. I prayed for the strength to take the medicine, even though it was awful. I prayed that my family wouldn't worry too much. I asked God for the wisdom to help me live well in whatever amount of time I had left. And God answered my prayers.

They were still very worried about their daughter. She was in pain, and they were in pain. But they stopped believing God was punishing them. They stopped imagining they had done something wrong. So we held hands and we prayed together. We asked God to give us the wisdom to take good care of their little girl. We prayed for the strength and courage to get through this terrible time with hope and love for one another. We prayed that she would know how much she is loved. And I think God answered their prayers, too.

Go to questions II

DO I HAVE TO GO TO A SYNAGOGUE TO PRAY?

"All right," Daniel conceded, *"so praying is cool. But do I have to go to synagogue to pray? Why can't I just go into the woods or out to the beach and talk with God?"*

You *can* go into the woods or out to the beach and talk with God. In fact, some of the best moments of prayer I've ever had were out in nature, far away from synagogues and services. You can go anywhere to pray.

The synagogue gives us a different experience of prayer. It is the experience of a community sharing prayer together and living life together.

Did you ever go to a baseball or football game? What's the difference between watching the game at the ballpark and watching the same game at home on TV? Unless you have really good seats, you probably see more on TV than from your seat in the ballpark. So why is the ballpark always a better experience? Because there's more than just the game going on. There's the game. And there's the crowd and their cheers, doing "the wave," screaming for the home team, and screaming at the other guys. There's the popcorn and the peanuts, the funny hats, those big foam fingers. It's the whole scene.

A synagogue service is to prayer what the afternoon at the ballpark is to the ball game. We pray, but we pray together. We blend our voices together in song. We share our lives with one another—happy moments and celebrations, as well as sad moments, tragedies, and the losses that come with life. We learn together—sharing our ideas about how life should be lived. When life is good, we share the joy. When life is difficult, we help one another find the courage not to give up, not to lose hope.

In the woods, I feel the presence of God in the peacefulness of the trees. At the beach, I feel the presence of God in the rhythm of the waves and the vastness of the ocean. In synagogue, I feel the presence of God in the sounds of all of us who have gathered to celebrate life together. In synagogue, I know that I belong—that my life matters to all these people. I am touched by the lives of others, and they are touched by me.

4

Talking Snakes and Splitting Seas ... Is Any of That Stuff in the Bible True?

Jennifer came to class early one afternoon. "I just had my first Bat Mitzvah lesson. I have to learn a whole section of the Torah, and then I have to talk about it in front everybody!" she said nervously. "Rabbi, do you really believe in all these stories? Does anyone? Are the stories in the Bible true?"

On the fourth Thursday in November, people in the United States gather together with their families and friends for a special feast. We eat turkey, stuffing, cranberry sauce, sweet potatoes, corn bread, and pumpkin pie. Before we eat all these wonderful foods, we tell a story. The story goes something like this:

In the year 1620, our Pilgrim ancestors left England, where they were persecuted, to find freedom in America. They sailed across the Atlantic Ocean on a ship called the *Mayflower* and landed in a cold, forbidding place: Massachusetts. Un-familiar with their surroundings, the Pilgrims starved. They would all have died had not the natives of that place come to help them. The natives taught the Pilgrims to grow local crops and hunt for game. With their help, the Pilgrims survived their first year and prospered in that place. After the next year's harvest, the Pilgrims held a feast to express gratitude to the natives for their help and to God for the gifts of survival and prosperity. And so we gather each year at this holiday of Thanksgiving to express our gratitude for the gifts of our lives.

We all know this story. But is it true?

Parts of it are true. The Pilgrims did come to America in 1620 on a ship called the *Mayflower*. They did settle in Plymouth, Massachusetts. They did have a tough time of it. And the natives did help them.

Parts of the story, on the other hand, aren't exactly fact.

For one thing, *my* ancestors weren't in Massachusetts in 1620. They were still in Eastern Europe. How can I talk about "my Pilgrim ancestors?"

For another, while the Pilgrims might have held a feast to thank the natives for their help, after dinner they pushed the natives aside and stole the continent from them! That part is somehow left out of our telling of the story.

Even if all the *facts* of the story aren't true, the *story* is still true. Because more than any other, this story tells us what it means to be an American.

To be an American is to tell this story in the first person—to say "my Pilgrim ancestors"—no matter where you came from and when you got here. Because all of us came here for the same reason: We were escaping from persecution and tyranny, looking for freedom.

Whether your ancestors landed at Plymouth, Massachusetts, Ellis Island in New York City, or San Francisco Bay, moving here was tough. Starting over in a new place takes tremendous courage. But somehow, we made it. And now we enjoy a special kind of life that is unique among the peoples of the world. Whatever our faith or religion, we understand the importance of taking a few moments each year to express gratitude for the gifts of America and for the privilege of living in this great land.

The most important part of the story is what our ancestors called themselves. They weren't the Refugees, or Immigrants, or Aliens, or Strangers. They called themselves Pilgrims. A pilgrim is someone who takes a journey to a special, sacred place. The story teaches us to look for what's special and sacred in America. That's what makes it a true story. We can understand Bible stories the same way. Bible stories are true, even if all the facts aren't accurate. Was there a Noah who built a boat and saved animals from a flood? We don't know. But the story is true: It teaches us that people can mess up the world by the choices they make, and people can save the world by the choices they make.

The Bible uses stories to teach us the most important truths of our lives.

Did all humanity come from one couple, Adam and Eve? Again, we don't know. But the story is true because it teaches us something very powerful: All human beings are one family. Therefore, all human beings are responsible for one another. People of other faiths, people with skin of a different color, people who live in other parts of the city or the nation or on the other side of the planet, people different from "us"—we are all part of the same family, and we are all responsible for one another.

It might be interesting to find out if the stories happened the way the Bible says they did. But the truth of a story is not in what happened a long time ago in a place far away. A story's truth is what it tells us about our lives right now. Can we find ourselves in the story?

Did a snake really convince Eve to eat the forbidden fruit? Personally, I haven't met many talking snakes. But I do know what it's like to be tempted to do something that I know is wrong. I know what that voice sounds like—and how hard it is to resist! What do you do when you hear that voice?

Was there a Moses who freed the Israelites from slavery? Did the ten plagues happen as the Torah tells us? Did the Red Sea really split?

If the story of the Pilgrims tells us what it means to be an American, the Passover story tells us what it means to be Jewish.

To be Jewish is to remember Egypt and all the other times in our history when we were slaves. What does it mean to be a slave? It means that we were treated not as people, not even as living creatures, but as objects. A slave is a person turned into a thing. We remember that, and we promise never to treat people that way; never to let anyone, anywhere be treated as a thing. We dream of a world where all people are treated as God's special creations. And we devote ourselves to making that dream come true. The ethics of the Jewish religion provide a way of making that dream come true.

To be Jewish is to remember what happened to Pharaoh. He thought he was a god and commanded people to worship him. In the end, however, his stubborn arrogance destroyed him.

To be Jewish is to remember Moses. One man, speaking the truth, was able to change history and free his people.

To be Jewish is to never give up hope. No matter how powerful evil may be, it can never destroy our dreams; it cannot enslave our imagination, our spirit, or our love. The Red Sea split. One day, all evil will drown itself and we will find ourselves on the road to the Promised Land.

The Bible tells us the most important truths about being alive. That's what makes it true.

IF GOD TALKED TO EVERYONE IN THE BIBLE, WHY DOESN'T GOD TALK TO ANYONE TODAY?

By now, the whole class had arrived, and everyone joined in Jennifer's discussion of Bible stories. Billy, who was still

searching for a way to believe in God, asked, "If God talked
to everyone in the Bible, why doesn't God talk to anyone
today?"

The Talmud, the great sourcebook of Judaism, was put
together about 1,500 years ago. There is a story in the
Talmud that I really love about the great Rabbis who lived
in the second century:

> The Rabbis were debating about a certain kind
> of oven. One of the greatest of the Rabbis,
> Rabbi Eliezer, gave every reason that the oven
> should be used. But the other Rabbis dis-
> agreed. Rabbi Eliezer wanted so badly to
> prove that he was right, he brought all kinds of
> miracles as proof. He made trees dance. He
> made a stream of water flow backward. He
> even made the walls of the academy start to
> fall over. The other Rabbis admired his ability
> to make miracles, but they answered, "In our
> discussion, miracles don't count as proof."
>
> Finally, Rabbi Eliezer said, "If I'm
> right, let God prove it!" And then, the Talmud
> tells us, the voice of God was heard to say:
> "Rabbi Eliezer is right! Why are you arguing
> with Rabbi Eliezer? He's always right!"
>
> At that moment, another great Rabbi,
> Rabbi Joshua, arose and responded: "The
> Torah is not in heaven!" (*Bava Metzia* 59b).

Rabbi Joshua was actually quoting the Torah. In Deuteronomy, Moses says to the People Israel, shortly before his death:

> This commandment I've given you today is not too difficult for you, nor is it far away. It is not in heaven, that you should say: "Who among us can go to the heavens and get it for us and give it to us that we may do it?" Neither is it beyond the sea, that you should say, "Who among us can cross to the other side of the sea and get it for us and teach it to us that we may do it?" No, it is very close to you, in your mouth and in your heart, to do it (Deuteronomy 30:11–14).

What did Rabbi Joshua mean by this? God gave us the Torah. And God gave us the responsibility to understand it and teach it. But if God were to show up every time we try and tell us we're wrong, we'll never get to do it ourselves. If God shows up each time, we'll never learn responsibility. To fulfill God's wish that we become responsible, God has to let us make our own decisions. In other words, Rabbi Joshua told God to back off!

There's a wonderful ending to this story. Some time later, there lived a rabbi, Rabbi Nathan, who was visited from time to time by the prophet Elijah. According to the Bible, Elijah never died; he was taken into heaven in a fiery chariot (II Kings 2:11–12). In the imagination of the Rabbis, Elijah lives forever, going around the world doing special things for special people and showing up at our seder tables each Pesach. When they met, Rabbi Nathan asked Elijah, "What did God do when Rabbi Joshua told God to back off?" Elijah answered, "He laughed with joy and said, 'My children have defeated me! My children have defeated me!'"

At some point, every mother and father have to back off and let kids do it their way (as long as they don't hurt themselves), even if they make mistakes. Otherwise, kids will never grow up and become responsible. There is a time for parents to tell kids what to do, and there's a time for parents to let kids assume responsibility.

If God keeps giving directions, we will never grow up. There is a time for God to speak, and there is a time for God to trust us to understand and be responsible.

God still speaks to us today. Not directly, but through the words of the Torah and the Prophets, the wisdom of the tradition, the symbols and rituals of our religion. When we think hard to understand the meaning of Torah and tradition, that's God's voice speaking through us. When we work hard making the dreams and ideals of the tradition part of our lives, that's God's voice showing us the way. When we teach others the wisdom of our tradition, that's God's voice teaching. Our sense of responsibility to God and to the Torah is an echo of the voice of God.

5

Why Does God Let Terrible Things Happen?

One afternoon at recess time everyone went outside for some fresh air, a snack, and a quick game of soccer—everyone except Molly. She just sat at her place looking dreamily out the window.

"Molly, are you OK?" I asked.

"I'm just depressed," she responded.

"Something going on? Anything I can do to help?"

"My aunt has cancer. She's probably going to die. My mom has been crying all week. And I don't know what to do or say to make her feel better." And Molly began to cry.

"Rabbi, sometimes life can be so hard. Why does God let such bad things happen?"

One Monday morning in January 1994, a powerful earthquake hit the northern sections of Los Angeles, where we lived. Our home was destroyed. It felt like the whole house went over a speed bump. Every window was shattered. Every wall crumbled. All our furniture fell over and most of our belongings were smashed. By some miracle, no one was hurt.

Some days later, the insurance company sent an inspector to look over the damage. He spent hours looking over the ruins of my house, and then he sat down to talk to us about our things. In the course of the conversation, he asked me what I did for a living. I told him I was a rabbi. He shook his head, "For a rabbi, your house sure took a beating! I thought God was supposed to take care of people like you!"

"God did take care of us," I answered, "He sent you!"

There are people who believe that everything that happens to them is God's decision. Everything, they believe, happens for a reason, even if only God knows the reason. If something good happens, they thank God. If something bad happens, they feel better thinking it was no accident. God brought this to them; therefore, it must be for the best. When bad things happen, they conclude that God is punishing them. All they need to do is figure out what they did wrong.

But if something really terrible happens, they might get angry and scream at God or give up on God. After all, they reason, if God is supposed to take care of them, how could this happen? What could they have done to deserve this? Like the family we talked about before, these poor people suffer three times as much: They suffer the bad things that have happened to them. And then they suffer double because they believe that they did something to deserve it; they think they're being punished. And they suf-

fer triple because most of the time, they can't figure out
what they did to deserve it. They feel guilt, they feel hurt,
and they feel God has abandoned them.

I don't agree with this way of thinking about God. I
don't believe that God decides everything that happens to
us. I don't believe that God punishes us with earthquakes
and diseases and accidents. I don't believe, for example,
that God sent the earthquake to destroy my house, or that
God sends diseases that destroy the lives of our loved ones.

In the Talmud there is a discussion of this question:

> Suppose a man stole a bag of seeds and
> planted them in his garden. What would hap-
> pen? It would be right if the seeds didn't
> grow! But nature follows its own rules, and
> the seeds grow. Suppose a man had rela-
> tions with his neighbor's wife. It would be
> right if she did not get pregnant. But nature
> follows its own rules, and she gets pregnant
> (*Avoda Zara* 54b).

Nature follows its own rules, and God doesn't stop
it. God doesn't break nature's rules.

According to nature's rules, the earth's crust moves,
and that causes earthquakes. It wasn't God's decision that
made the earth shake and wreck all the houses on my
street. And God didn't break nature's rule just because a
rabbi lived on the block. My house was wrecked, too.

So, where was God?

Some amazing things happened in the days following the earthquake. Right after the shaking stopped, there was a loud knock at my door. It was my neighbors, checking to make sure everyone was safe. They were afraid we were hurt or trapped and brought tools, lanterns, and first aid.

For three days following the quake, we stayed in the wrecked shell of our house to pack our things and get ready to move. During that time there was no water, no gas, and no electricity. We had to buy bottled water, but everywhere we went to get it, the price was doubled or tripled. One afternoon, a big yellow truck pulled onto our block. A guy and his son were selling water—for even less than the regular price. When I asked him why, he explained that he lived in another town that was unaffected by the quake. He saw the terrible damage on the TV news and wanted to help, so he and his young son rented this truck, bought all the bottled water they could find, and brought it out to us. He was just glad he could help. He was glad he could show his son how to help. Where was God in the earthquake? Maybe God was in the strong hands of my neighbors, or in the kind generosity of the man in the yellow truck.

God isn't the cause of tragedy. Tragedy happens because we live in nature, and nature includes earthquakes and diseases. You can find God in our courage to get through and in our willingness to share kindness and support to survive the tragedy.

How Can Anyone Believe in
After the Holocau.

Recess was over, and everyone came in to join our discussion.

"We've been reading The Diary of Anne Frank *in my English class," Jennifer related. "I just keep thinking about how unfair it is that she was killed in the concentration camp and never got to grow up."*

"My grandma was in the Holocaust," reported Daniel. "She has these numbers on her arm. But she never talks about it."

"Rabbi," asked Molly, "what about the Holocaust? How can anyone believe in God after the Holocaust?"

The Holocaust is the worst tragedy in all of human history. The evil of the Holocaust is so horrible that there are no words to describe it. Saying "6 million Jews were murdered" or "11 million innocent people died" cannot begin to convey how terrible this was. If every individual human life is precious and irreplaceable, how can one even imagine 6 million or 11 million?

How do we find God after a tragedy as huge as the Holocaust? This may be the hardest question for any religious person today.

One who believes that God decides what happens to every human being cannot answer this question. How could there be a reason for the destruction of 6 million Jews, including 1 million Jewish children? It's no wonder that many people stopped believing in God after the Holocaust.

Remember the Talmud's teaching. God doesn't stop nature from following its own rules. Human beings have a nature. The most important part of human nature is our ability to make choices. We can choose to be good or evil, to do good or evil. We choose to be loving or hateful, to build or to destroy. And just as God doesn't interfere when nature follows its own rules, God doesn't stop human beings from making their own choices. Even when they choose the worst of evil.

Human beings chose to build the concentration camps and the gas chambers and to murder millions. That was a human choice, not God's decision.

But God was not entirely absent from the Holocaust. God didn't check out. Just as in the earthquake, God was present wherever human beings found the ability to resist the evil, to overcome the pain, to share kindness and care, and to get through the tragedy.

I'm sure you've heard of Hitler. You may even know the names of Himmler, Goering, and Goebbels. These were the leaders of the Nazis. But have you ever heard of Joop Westerweel, Sempo Sugihara, and Raul Wallenberg? Do you know who they were?

The Nazis enlisted thousands of people to help them murder the Jews of Europe. Millions of others stood by and ignored it all and let it happen. (After the war they claimed, "We didn't know what was going on.") But there were others, very few, who resisted. They were not Jewish, but they risked their lives to save Jews from the Nazis.

Joop Westerweel was a Dutch teacher who organized an "underground railroad," leading small groups of Jews by bicycle out of Holland, all the way across France, and into Spain, a neutral country where Jews were safe. He saved dozens of Jews. In 1944, he was caught by the Nazis. They killed him for saving Jewish lives.

Sempo Sugihara was a Japanese ambassador stationed in Lithuania. When the Nazis invaded that country, the Jews were trapped. The Nazis were on one side eager to kill them. On the other side were the Russians, who wouldn't let them in. Russia would open its border and let the Jews in only if they had special visas—like passports—showing that they were on their way to somewhere else. But no country would give them these visas. Finally, in desperation, the Jews came to Sugihara and begged him for help. Sugihara's superiors in Tokyo told him not to help the Jews, but he ignored that order. He saw the fear in the eyes of these Jews and he knew that he had to help. Sugihara began writing visas for Jews. With the help of his wife and son, Sugihara wrote 3,500 visas in one night, saving more than 10,000 Jewish lives.

Raul Wallenberg was a diplomat from Sweden assigned to the Swedish embassy in Budapest, Hungary. He was shocked at what the Nazis were doing to Jews. He set up a special zone in Budapest, under the direction of the

Red Cross, where Jews were safe from the Nazis. Wallenberg worked tirelessly bringing Jews to safety, sometimes even pulling them off the trains that would have taken them to the concentration camps. By the end of the war, Wallenberg had saved 30,000 Jews. At the war's end, he disappeared. It is believed that he was arrested by the Soviets and died in a Soviet prison.

Westerweel, Sugihara, and Wallenberg were not Jewish. But they risked their lives—some even gave up their lives—to save Jews from the Nazis. And they were not alone. In every country where the Nazis tried to kill Jews, there were people who risked their own lives to save Jewish lives. These were just ordinary people—farmers, fisherman, Catholic priests and Protestant ministers, teachers, and government officials—who did the right thing. Compared to the thousands who helped the Nazis or the millions who watched and did nothing, these heroes were very few in number, maybe a few thousand. But because of them, we can believe that God was still alive even in the most terrible of places at the most terrible of times.

Bad things happen to us because nature treats us all the same. The earth shakes, and all our homes are destroyed. Our bodies fail, and we get sick. Bad things happen to us because human beings choose to do evil. Sometimes entire nations choose evil, and a Holocaust destroys millions of innocent lives. Bad things happen, but God didn't make them happen. God doesn't punish us in that way.

That doesn't mean that God is absent. Even in the very worst of circumstances, God is present in our ability to overcome and survive, in our ability to share caring and help. God is present in our ability to transform the world— bringing kindness where there was hate, bringing healing where there was pain, bringing hope where there was despair. When we witness tragedy and pain, the real question isn't, Where was God? The real question is, Where are you? What is your response or responsibility if people suffer and the world is ugly?

There is an old story:

A man who goes up to heaven at the end of his life. He stands before the throne of God. The man looks up at God and says, "You know, I'm very angry at You! Can't You see that the world You created is filled with suffering and ugliness and destruction? Why don't You do something to fix the world's mess?"

God looks down at the man, and in a gentle voice says, "I did do something. I sent you."

6

What Is God Anyway?

Josh knew sports. In the world of sports, he was a genius. He could cite from memory statistics, records, and the important moments of championship games. When anything else was discussed, he checked out, preferring to sketch sports heroes to participating in our discussions. So it came as a complete surprise one afternoon when his hand went up and, with all the confidence of a boxing champ, he entered the ring.

"We've been talking about God. God, God, God. I still don't believe in God!"

"That's OK. I'm glad to see you're thinking about it," I responded. "Tell me something, what do you mean by the word 'God?'"

He didn't expect this response. "What do you mean, what do I mean by 'God'? You're a rabbi; you know what God is!"

"Well, you've told me you're not sure about God. I just

want to be sure I understand what you don't believe. What do you mean by the word 'God'?"

Josh tried to answer. "Most people would say that God is an invisible spirit who lives in heaven and rewards good people and punishes evil people. I just can't believe in that."

He looked at me the way you look at a teacher to see if you got the right answer on the quiz.

"Josh, it's not God you don't believe in," I told him. "It's Santa Claus. Santa Claus brings presents to the good kids and coal to the bad ones. Your problem isn't with God. Because if that's what God is supposed to be, then I don't believe in God, either."

Now he was the one who was shocked. "But you're the rabbi. You've got to believe!"

"Don't I get to believe in something that makes sense to me?" I replied.

When I was a child, I believed that God was a grand-fatherly fellow who lived invisibly in heaven and took care of me. I suspect that many people start out with this same idea. As I got older, my ideas about God changed. As we grow more sophisticated, it's important that our ideas of God do also. Otherwise, we get stuck with childish ideas of God and religion that don't fit us any more than the clothes and shoes we wore as little kids. Searching, questioning, debating, trying out different ideas about God is the way we grow religiously.

Here is a way to think about God. When you look at

yourself in a mirror, what do you see? You see yourself, right? You see your face, your arms, your shoulders, and your chest. If it's a big mirror, maybe you see your legs and feet. You see your body. But is that you? Is it all of you? Where's your personality? Your sense of humor? The things you know? Your interests and abilities? Can you see that in the mirror?

What's missing from the mirror image? You see your body, but you don't see that part of you we call your "self." And no matter how good-looking you are, your "self" part is much more important! It's the part that makes you ... you! Lots of people have arms and legs. But only you have this "self."

But what is this "self?" What's it made of? Where is it? How did it get here? Isn't it strange that the "self," which is the essence of you, is so hard to describe? It's so close, but it's hard to find words to define it.

Suppose we look at the world in the same way. Imagine the universe—the earth, the stars and planets, all of nature, everything that is, was, and ever will be—like a body. Is there a "self" living in this body?

God is the "self" of the universe.

Just as it is impossible to describe and define your own "self," it is impossible to describe and define God.

In the Torah, God has a personal name. In Hebrew this name is spelled *Yud-Hay-Vav-Hay*. When we see this name, we say "Adonai," which means "my master." But the name itself can't be pronounced. Why a name you can't say? You can only name things that can be defined or described. If you can't define it or describe it, it is difficult to name it. The fuzzier the definition, the fuzzier its name becomes. God, the "self" of the universe, can't be defined. So God's name can't be pronounced.

Even though we can't define God, there are things we can say. We can say what difference it makes to us knowing that God is in the universe.

Look into the mirror again. You've got arms, legs, hair, feet. Each part is different, but they are all one person because they are all part of your "self." The floor you're standing on, the clothes you're wearing, and your shoes aren't part of your "self." It's this sense of "self" that makes your parts into one person. Similarly, to say that the universe has a "self" is to say that everything is *one*. And so we say the *Shema*, the most important prayer in Jewish religion: Hear O Israel, Adonai is God, Adonai is One. The important word is the last word: *One*.

When we're talking about God, we're not talking about someone being up there in heaven, somebody separate from us and from the world, looking down on us. God isn't "up there," or even "out there." God is the All. God is everything. God is what connects everything to everything else. Including us, the ones looking for God.

When we say the *Shema*, our most important prayer, we are saying that God—the All—is not broken up into two, or three, or more. The world can't be divided. You can't say, "This is my place and this is yours," or "These are our

people and those are others." You can't divide humanity
into "us" and "them." We're all one. We're all connected. If I
hurt you, I hurt myself. So Torah commands me to love my
neighbor as myself (Leviticus 19:18). My neighbor and me,
we're really one.

Imagine a wave on the ocean. Now imagine that
God is the ocean and each of us is a wave. A wave is part
of the ocean. A wave rises up out of the ocean to become
distinct, and then it goes back again. Now, suppose the
wave became aware of itself. It might think it was a separate, independent being. What would it take to make the
wave discover that it was part of the ocean? And then how
would it feel? How would that discovery change the wave's
idea of itself? The wave would know that in reality, it was
connected to every other wave. It would know that after it
had risen and then fallen back into the sea, it wasn't really
gone but would rise again as another wave. It would
understand that in reality, it was much, much bigger than
just one wave.

What difference does this idea of God make in real
life?

Most people behave as if they were astronauts. Like
astronauts, they think they live in a sealed suit, in a sealed
capsule, isolated and insulated from the environment
around them. Their space suit is their skin, and inside is
what they call "me." When we say we feel close to God, we
are recognizing the truth that we're not astronauts. We're
not isolated beings. We are part of our environment, part of

our community, part of our world. And it's all part of us. Because we're all part of God and God is One.

The problem is, we constantly forget this truth. We forget and we start to think and behave like astronauts, as if nothing we do affects anyone else or the world around us. The most important purpose of religion is to remind us constantly that we are part of the All. That's how our belief in God leads directly to a sense of being responsible for the world.

WHAT'S THAT ABOUT GOD BEING A SHEPHERD ... ARE WE SUPPOSED TO BE SHEEP?

"OK, Rabbi," Josh continued, "but there's this line in the prayer book about God being a shepherd. What's that about? Are we supposed to be sheep? Baaaaa!"

Think again about your "self." What is it? Is it a thing? If we took you apart, piece by piece, we'd find your heart, your lungs, your brain. Would we find your "self?" The self isn't a thing that we touch and look at. If I want to know your "self," or if you want to know mine, how can we do that? I get to know you by listening to what you say. I watch how you act. From the things you do and say I get a sense of what's important to you. Soon I can say that I know you. Every one of us has a unique pattern of behaving that identifies us. If you were to start behaving strangely, we might say, "You're not yourself today." Your unique pattern of behavior is your "self." Self is not a thing, but a pattern of action. With God it works the same way.

In the Torah, Moses asks God our question. He says, "Let me see Your presence." And God responds: "I will make all my goodness pass before you, and I will proclaim before you the name of the Lord, and the grace I will grant and the compassion I will show, but you cannot see my face, for man may not see me and live" (Exodus 33:17–20). Moses is God's closest friend. He wants to know what we want to know: What is God? God tells him, You can't know that. What you can know is what I do in the world, how I love the world and care for the world. Moses accepts this because he understands that knowing God is not a matter of knowing what God is, but what God does.

In the prayer book, we find lots of words describing God—Shepherd, Father, King, Rock, Healer, Redeemer. But these aren't meant to be literally true. God isn't really a shepherd herding sheep around. God isn't really a rock. These are metaphors. A metaphor, you will remember from English class, describes something by comparing it to something else. To unlock a metaphor, we need to find the common idea beneath the metaphor and what it refers to.

What does it mean to say, "God is a Shepherd"? Just as a shepherd takes care of the sheep, we have a sense that God takes care of us. God is a Father. Just as parents love their kids, protect them, and provide for them, we have a sense that God loves us, protects us, and provides for us. God is King. Just as a monarch sets the rules of an empire, we believe that God gives us the rules for living a good life.

Our religion is full of metaphors for God. But notice what these metaphors tell us: They don't tell us what God *is*, they tell us what God *does*. They describe the pattern of God's actions.

Perhaps we should change the way we talk about God. What if we used the word God not as a noun, but as a verb or an adverb? Using God as a noun is confusing. It makes us think of God as the name of something that we can see and touch. We imagine God as a giant person living up in heaven. Or we describe God in confusing words like "spirit" or "power" or "being."

Perhaps a better way to use the word God is as a verb or an adverb, like "God-ing" or "acting Godly." When we say "God," we're not talking about a person or a thing or a being, we're talking about a pattern of events in the world and in our lives, or about a quality of an action or a moment.

If God is a noun, a thing, we keep asking, What is God? or Where is God? But once we start thinking of God as a verb or an adverb, we can ask different questions. With verbs we can ask When and How questions, like When is God? When are we acting Godly? How can we do God in the world?

Our religion is our way of answering these questions. Our religion helps us find the God that's happening all around us. Our religion teaches us what is the Godly pattern of acting in our world, and what is not. Judaism is an invitation to join in acting Godly, in doing God. When we say that we feel close to God, we are saying that we are involved in God, participating in God, living Godly.

When the film *The Prince of Egypt* was being made, I had a friend at the studio who invited me to see an early version of the film and to meet the director. The filmmakers had a problem: When Moses hears God's voice at the burning bush, what does God sound like? Should God sound like Darth Vader? Should God's voice be a man's voice or a woman's voice? A gentle voice or an angry voice? I remembered that this same question was discussed by the ancient Rabbis. The Rabbis came up with an astonishing answer: The voice Moses heard was his own voice. And that's how it turned out in the film! When Moses hears God's voice from the burning bush, it's his own voice commanding him to go and free his people. God's voice doesn't come from far away. If we're part of God, God can speak to us from the deepest part of ourselves. The great problem is learning to listen.

The Bible's very first chapter says that God created the human being "in God's image." What does this mean? Perhaps it teaches that if we want to find God, we need not look up to heaven or out into the universe. The closest place to find God is within each of us. When I pray, I'm not praying "up" to God who lives in heaven. I'm looking deep within myself, trying to find the parts of me that best reflect God.

When I hear God, it's not like the booming voice of a loudspeaker coming from above, but the voice of the deepest part of me pleading for me to live a more Godly life.

When God acts in the world, it's not through thunder-and-lightning miracles from the sky. It's through the selfless acts of people like Charles, who heal and help.

7

What's the Meaning of Life? Is That a Dumb Question?

WHAT'S LIFE FOR?

Everyone in the class came in very excited.

"You'll never guess who came to school today!" exclaimed Ashley, who is our class film, TV, and music critic.

"Who?" I responded, clueless.

She waited a dramatic second, and then rolled out a name.

"Who's that?" I asked. Honestly, I'd never heard the name.

"What universe to do you live in?" asked Ashley, rolling her eyes with exasperation. "He's just the hottest star of the greatest show that's ever been on TV. How could you not know?!"

"Is he important?"

"He's gorgeous! He's famous! And he's probably rich. What else is there?"

"Is he important?" I tried again.

"What's important got to do with it? Isn't being rich and

famous and beautiful enough for one life? Isn't that what everyone wants?"

"But is it worth wanting? Will it really make you happy?"

Ashley, who has spent a good part of her life studying the lives and loves of celebrities, now begins to reflect. "Rabbi, can I ask you a dumb question? What else is there besides becoming rich and famous? What's life for? What's the meaning of life?"

Why is this a dumb question? I think it's about the most important question you can ask.

Asking this question means you're taking life seriously. You're asking, What's worth caring about? What's worth worrying about? What's worth working for? What's going to give me the greatest satisfaction? What will make me happiest in life? Would being rich and famous make us happy? Would it give us a life that matters?

Some years ago, someone gave my family a gift: a year's subscription to *People* magazine. At first I laughed at this. What a trashy, gossipy, awful excuse for a magazine. But as I read *People*, I discovered that it has a great wisdom to teach. *People* magazine has pages and pages about rich, famous, and beautiful people ... and how utterly miserable they are. They do drugs. They can't stay married to the same person for more than a few minutes. Their kids hate them. They have no friends. And they're always worried about losing it all. For all their riches, fame, and beauty, these people aren't happy.

The Talmud has a remarkable teaching:

"Without bread, there's no Torah. And without
Torah, there's no bread" (*Pirke* Avot 3:17).

The first part, I understand. People who are starving think about nothing else but their starvation. Torah is the last thing on your mind when you're really hungry.

It's the second part that is really interesting. If you have no Torah—if you have no bigger purpose in life, no idea what life is for—then what good is having tons of money?

The world we live in, according to an old Jewish tradition, is broken. Our world is filled with jagged edges and shattered pieces. We touch the world's broken-ness in all the evils we meet in the world—disease, violence, hate, war, hunger, poverty, and ignorance.

The world needs repair. God has invited us to share the work of repairing the world. That's what the Bible means when it says we have a "covenant" with God. We are God's partners. Our job is to repair the world. The world that we meet is a mixture of order and mess, of good and evil, of darkness and light. It is our job, as God's partners, to bring order to the mess, to bring good out of evil, to cast light into the darkness. God needs us. God has a dream of a whole, unbroken, finished world. God needs our help to fulfill that dream.

Imagine being important enough to be God's partner! What a huge honor! What a huge responsibility!

No one has the power to do the whole job alone. You

need help from friends, teachers, and allies. But neither can you run away from your responsibility. You are needed.

There is a corner of the world that is yours. It is broken, and only you can fix it. It is a mess, and only you can make it beautiful. You were created with a special blend of abilities to do this job. You must find that corner and apply to it all your energies, talents, imagination, and intelligence. That's your mission. That's your purpose. And that's the meaning of your life.

"But Rabbi," Ashley tried to persuade me, "he's my hero! He's a star! He's so famous! Wouldn't it be great to be famous?"

Does being famous make you a hero?

Erin Brockovich saved the people of a whole town from the poison a local factory was dumping in their water. They made a movie about her life, and Julia Roberts played her in the movie. A billion or so people saw Julia Roberts win the Oscar for playing Erin Brockovich. What award did Erin Brockovich win for saving those people? Everyone knows what Julia Roberts looks like. She's famous. Does anyone know what Erin Brockovich looks like? I didn't. I met Erin Brockovich. I stood on line behind her in the supermarket. I didn't know who she was until the clerk asked her for her driver's license when she wrote a check. (I guess he didn't know who she was, either.) Isn't it strange who becomes famous? Given the choice, do you think most people would rather be Erin Brockovich, or Julia Roberts—the person who saved a whole town, or the actor who played her in the movie? Who is the real hero?

I've met heroes in my life.

Jonathan was the smartest kid in my Hebrew School class. After graduating high school, he went off to a big Ivy League college. We were all really proud of him. A couple of years ago, I found my old friend again. He's a doctor working in research. He could have been very, very rich, but he's made a different choice. He spends all his time searching for the way to cure cancer and AIDS. He's got an army of scientists and researchers working with him in a major university laboratory. If he's successful, he may win a Nobel Prize. But that's not why he works so hard. He just wants to find the cures that will restore life to those who suffer.

Mark was the worst student in Hebrew School. The very, very worst. And his life only went down from there. He became a criminal and a drug addict. Eventually, he ended up in state prison. But something told him he could do more. When he got out of prison, he helped set up a center for kids who were in trouble. He teaches that every person can change his or her life, that each person can lift himself or herself up to a life of goodness. This is what Judaism calls *Teshuva*. Mark is a champion of *Teshuva*. Mark helps kids to get free of drugs and to stay away from crime. He teaches them to live decent, good lives—lives that matter. He has saved hundreds of kids who would have been destroyed by their bad choices.

You couldn't find two men as different as Jonathan and Mark. They are my heroes. Each has found the corner of the world he is uniquely responsible for. And each gives his heart and soul to fixing that corner. Each lives a life that matters. Each has found the meaning of his life. You can, too.

8

No Cheeseburgers?
No Going to the Mall
on Saturday? Why Does
Religion Need So
Many Rules?

Michael arrived with a bag of fast food.

"Michael, I'm sorry," I tell him, "but you can't eat that here. It's the rules."

"What kind of crazy rules?!" He's frustrated. But he gets the question. "Why does religion need to have so many rules? What's God got against cheeseburgers?"

Once, long ago, I joined a gym. Along with my new membership came one session with a trainer. His name was Bobby. Bobby had muscles on his muscles. He looked like he'd spent his life in the gym. Bobby talked to me about all the good things exercise could do for me. He took me through a workout and showed me how to use all the exercise machines in the gym. He taught me how to put together a program that would get me into shape. Then he asked me a very simple question: "How often can you get here?"

He continued, "Can you make it five days a week?"

"I'm pretty busy," I said. "That's going to be hard."

"OK," he said, "four days a week?"

"I don't know," I replied.

"Three days a week?" He was looking worried.

"I'm not sure; my schedule is pretty tight."

"Two days? Once a week?" I shook my head.

"Well," Bobby concluded, "you're not ready to be serious, are you? And if you're not serious," he warned me, "you can't do this right. You can't just wish yourself a new body; you have to do something. You have to do something every single day to make it happen. Come back when you're ready to be serious."

Bobby was right. If I really wanted results, I needed to be serious, which meant putting in some real time in the gym. And that would mean making some real changes in the way I live my life.

Maybe Bobby was a prophet. He asked the question the Torah might ask us: "Are you ready to be serious?" You say you want to be a better person. You say you want to make the world a better place. Doing these things requires changing ourselves and the way we live. That's hard work. It means doing something every day. That's why our religion has so many rules. Like Bobby's exercises, the rules set out the ways we make ourselves better and make our world better every day. But they work only if we're serious.

Let's start with cheeseburgers.

If you read the first chapters of the Bible, you will discover that human beings were supposed to be vegetarians (see Genesis 1:29 and 2:15). In the Garden of Eden, we ate only fruits and vegetables. We lived in peace with nature. Animals didn't fear us, and the world was without conflict and violence. That was God's dream. But humans had other ideas. We wanted to eat meat.

Let's remember something: Eating meat means killing something. We tend to forget this because our meat comes all nicely wrapped from the market or served on a bun with pickles and ketchup at McDonald's. But before it reached the market or the restaurant, that burger was a living, breathing creature that someone had to kill. There's violence involved in the eating of meat.

One ancient Rabbi suggested that anyone who really wants to eat meat should have to kill the animal himself or herself. Think about that. If you really wanted a burger, they'd bring you the animal and a sharp knife, and you'd have to look the animal in the eye and do the killing yourself. Sounds gross? That was the Rabbi's point. If it's disgusting to imagine killing the animal ourselves, why is it less gross if someone else does it for us?

Although God dreamed that we'd be vegetarians, God recognized that people want meat. The laws of *kashrut*, keeping kosher, are God's compromise. Their purpose is to let us kill animals for food but preserve our love and respect for life. Kill animals if you must, but don't become a killer.

Many people make the mistake of thinking that the laws of *kashrut* are intended to keep us healthy. Keeping healthy is also a mitzvah, a commandment of God, but that's not the purpose of *kashrut*. You can eat a very healthy non-kosher diet and a very unhealthy kosher one. The real purpose has to do with the value of life and controlling our power to kill.

If you're a vegetarian, you automatically keep kosher. But if you eat meat or fish, there are four basic laws of *kashrut*:

1. Only certain animals may be eaten. There is nothing really special about the choice of which animals we eat and which we don't. God didn't make pigs and lobsters forbidden because they are more beloved than cows and salmon. Nor are they any cleaner or more holy. The idea is that we're not allowed to go out and just kill whatever we feel like killing. Our killing is limited to a specific list of permitted animals.

2. The animal must be killed in the most painless way possible. Even an animal designated for our food has feeling. You may kill to eat, but you may not allow the animal to suffer.

3. All the blood must be removed from the meat. Blood symbolizes life because blood is always moving in a living body and provides life to the organism. All life belongs to God. You may eat the animal,

but you must not imagine that you created the life of this animal.

4. All foods made from milk and all foods made from meat must be prepared, served, and eaten separately. Meat, which involves killing, symbolizes the taking of life. Milk, which nourishes newborns, symbolizes the giving of life. The two must never be confused in our lives.

In keeping milk and meat separate, we are taught that our real tasks are to limit our desire to destroy life, and to develop our abilities to give life. This is something our culture badly needs to learn. Think about movies, for example. How many movies contain terrible violence—killing people, hurting people, blowing things up—and we just laugh and have a great time? Is there something wrong here? Should violence and death be considered entertainment? Should violence and death be fun to watch?

What's wrong with a cheeseburger? First, we don't know how the animal was killed. Were those who killed the animal careful that the animal didn't suffer? Or did they just kill it the easiest way, even if it hurt the animal? Second, we don't know if they drained out the blood. Most animals we eat were raised on huge ranches and killed in huge factories where no one ever cares that they are living creatures. Finally, cheese, which is made from milk, is mixed up with meat. Life is mixed up with death. Violence is mixed up with pleasure. Saying no to a cheeseburger is a way of saying no to a world that mixes up life and death, violence and fun.

The rules of *kashrut* keep us thinking about the preciousness of life and God's dream of a peaceful world. Every time we pick up a fork and wonder if it is for milk or meat, we are awakened to the ancient dream of a world free of violence.

Michael stuffed his fast-food bag into his desk, but he was ready with another question.

"OK, now I understand the rules about food, but what's this about not going to the mall on Saturday? That's the best day to go to the mall!"

Have you ever see those stories on TV about the people who won the lottery? One day this guy wakes up, and he's a multimillionaire. Ever wonder how your life would change if you were suddenly a multimillionaire? Suddenly, you wouldn't have to worry about earning a living anymore. You'd have more than enough. You'd be free. You'd work only if you wanted to. You'd get to live on your own terms, do whatever you wanted. So what would you do? Would you continue in school? Would you take a job? Would you do art? Make music? Travel the world?

Do you know what's amazing about those stories of people who win the lottery? It's how unhappy so many of them are. All that money, all the possibilities, all the freedom, and they don't know what to do with it. These are people who have spent their entire lives dreaming of being rich and free. Now they've got it—and it drives them crazy! They don't know how to be free. They don't know what to do with their new freedom.

In the Torah, Moses takes the People Israel out of Egypt, out of slavery. But the Israelites keep trying to go back. They want to trade in freedom for slavery because they don't know how to be free. They don't know what to do with it.

I probably won't ever win a lottery. I'll probably never be a multimillionaire. But once a week, for one whole day, I pretend I'm one. I spend one day a week doing what I'd do if I won the lottery. I spend one day a week being free. To do this right, I've had to spend some serious time thinking about what to do with my freedom. What's most important to me?

The rules of Judaism teach me, first, what to do with my freedom. And second, they keep me from "going back to Egypt"—from ditching freedom and going back to be a slave.

The rules of Shabbat teach me that family, friends, and community are important. So I spend Shabbat with my family, my friends, and my community. During the work-week, I'm awfully busy. I don't listen to my family and my friends as I should. I don't hear about their lives, their discoveries, their joy. On Shabbat, I take time to listen.

The rules of Shabbat teach me that our ability to enjoy the beauty of nature is one of God's gifts. So I spend part of each Shabbat enjoying nature. I treat nature the way we would treat an artistic masterpiece: I appreciate it, but I don't try to change it. During my workweek, I'm always trying to change things—I'm trying to make things better. On Shabbat, I leave things alone and enjoy them as they are.

The rules of Shabbat teach me to find joy in the moments of my life. On this special day, I don't need possessions to make me happy. Life makes me happy. That's why I stay away from the mall on Shabbat. The mall is all about shopping. The mall says, "The way to be happy is to buy new stuff. You need this new outfit! You need this new makeup! You need this new music!" But Shabbat answers, "Be happy with what you've got! More stuff won't make you happier! Only living better can make you happy!"

All week long, I'm running around getting things done. On Shabbat, I can slow down and really live. On Shabbat, I'm a millionaire, enjoying the freedom I've earned and taking pleasure in the gifts of my life.

> Michael isn't convinced. "But Rabbi, what difference does it make if you keep these rules? Is the world going to change if I give up cheeseburgers?"

I know that refusing a cheeseburger is not going to end all the violence in the world. And I know that staying away from the mall on Shabbat is not going to change the belief that stuff makes you happy. My choices may change the world just a little, but they will change *me* a lot. If I'm going to help repair the world, I have to begin by repairing myself. I have to fix the broken parts of me—my violence, my hate, my greed, and my jealousy. I have to live differently, think differently, and look at the world differently. That's the purpose of these rules.

The word for *rule* in Judaism is *mitzvah*. A mitzvah is, literally, God's commandment, God's rule. A mitzvah is God's tool in shaping human beings. A mitzvah teaches me to see the world through God's eyes. A mitzvah teaches me my power to work with God in repairing myself and repairing the world. A mitzvah is a way of teaching me to act Godly.

Keeping kosher is a mitzvah. It teaches me to feel God's love for every living creature.

Observing Shabbat is a mitzvah. It teaches me the preciousness of every moment of time.

Tzedaka, giving charity, is a mitzvah that teaches me the true importance and power of money.

Putting a mezuzah on my door is a mitzvah that teaches me that my home can be a place of holiness.

Judaism has many, many mitzvot, because Judaism's job is ultimately to teach us how to live an important life, how to live with seriousness and with purpose, how to share God's dreams, how to repair ourselves and the world. That's our goal. It's something we work at every day, if we're serious. Just ask Bobby.

9

What Do You See
When You Look at Me?

*I came into the class one afternoon to find all the boys huddled
in the corner around Brian's desk.*

*"Rabbi, you've got to come see this!" they shouted. I guess
it's good to be one of the guys. So I went over to see what was so
fascinating.*

"Rabbi, can you believe this?!"

It seems that Brian had intercepted a Victoria's Secret
*catalog from the family mail and brought it to Hebrew School.
"Whoa! Is she hot or what?!"*

*"That is so gross!" moaned the girls from the other side of
the room, "How can you let them do that, Rabbi?"*

*"What's wrong with it?" challenged Josh, "They're just pic-
tures!" Then Josh turned a bit reflective and asked me, "Is there
anything wrong with it, Rabbi?"*

The question is, what do you see when you look at pictures
like that? You're looking at a human being, but you're seeing

only their surfaces, their outsides. You don't see a human being; you see a pretty object. Soon enough, these pictures train you to look at real people as objects.

Unfortunately, it's very common for men to look at a woman and notice the shape of her body and the features of her face, and that's all. They forget that there's a person, a self, inside that body and behind that face. They forget that this is a person with her own talents, interests, dreams, and goals—and not just a shapely body and pretty face. And what's even worse is that girls and women begin to look at themselves the same way, evaluating themselves only by their looks. They begin to feel that they're not thin enough, not pretty enough, and therefore not good enough.

The Torah teaches that God created the human being in God's own image, *tzelem eloheem*. This doesn't mean that God looks like us. It means that we carry certain qualities of God—the ability to create, to reason, to care. This is the strongest way the Torah could express the preciousness of each human being and the most powerful way it could demand that we value each person's uniqueness. The second of the Ten Commandments prohibits the making of images of God. So there is only one way to see an image of God in the world: in the character of each human being. When you see a human being, what you're to see is not just a face or a body, and not a pretty object, but a reflection of God.

This includes yourself. Without becoming conceited, it is very important for each of us to recognize how special and important we are. The Rabbis of the Talmud asked: If God wanted to fill the world with people, why in Genesis did God create only one human being? Why not create whole cities and civilizations? They answered: To teach the infinite preciousness and absolute uniqueness of each human being. How precious?

> One who destroys a single life, the Torah considers it as if he destroyed the entire world. And one who saves but a single life, the Torah considers it as if he saved an entire world.... This is an example of the greatness of God. For a human being mints coins with a single stamp, and they all come out looking the same. But God mints all human beings with the stamp of the first man, and yet each is unique. Therefore, every single human being must say, "For my sake, was the whole world created" (*Sanhedrin* 37a).

"Come on, Rabbi, lighten up," Jason complained. "We're just guys having some fun!"

Teenage boys—and even older guys—find pictures like that exciting. It's the way you're wired. But just because you're wired that way doesn't mean you must *behave* that way. You have a higher self—a conscience, the values you've been taught, your internal sense of what's right. And as much as your wiring makes you want to do something, you have the power to choose otherwise.

The Talmud teaches, "Who is strong? One who conquers his impulses" (*Pirke Avot* 4:1). This was written at the time when Roman gladiators fought in arena battles and Roman legions conquered the world. But the Talmud understood that the greatest strength is the strength to control yourself, and the greatest conquest is the conquest of your drives and desires.

Notice, however, that it doesn't say, "One who has no impulses." The Rabbis understood how we're wired. They knew that God created us that way. There are religions that teach that the body and its desires are the source of evil. Not Judaism: In Jewish teaching, the body is a creation of God. The body's impulses and desires aren't evil, but neither are they good. It depends on what you do with them. We have to learn a way not to destroy our impulses but to channel them. We have to learn how to make them expressions of the highest part of ourselves.

Drinking wine can make a person drunk. Or, we can make wine into a symbol of a family gathered to celebrate Shabbat or a holiday, and it becomes kiddush.

Eating just for the sake of eating is what animals do. Or, we can make a meal a time of sharing and caring and it becomes a holy meal.

Craving money can destroy a person's life and the life of a family. Or, we can use money to repair the world and transform it into *tzedaka*.

Sexual desire, like all the other drives, can poison and destroy a person's life. Or, we can turn it into a symbol of the love, responsibility, and commitment two people share.

It's all a question of how you see yourself. You are a body. But you are not only a body. You carry God's image with you, and you have the power to turn your life into a reflection of God in the world.

10

Why Are There So Many Different Religions? Aren't They All the Same?

"I went to a church last week with my friend from school,"
reported Michelle, a very serious and studious young woman.

"How was it?" I asked her.

"Very, very interesting. Some things were just like our reli-
gion, and some things were very different. Why are there so
many different religions? Aren't all religions the same?"

When I was growing up, I worried that my family wasn't "normal" because we were nothing like the families on TV. Back
then, TV families all sat down to eat together in peace, listening to one another in quiet conversation. My family was nothing
like that. When we sat down to eat, we were loud: talking, arguing, telling jokes, and sharing stories. Loud! When my Dad
asked us what we were learning in school, he really wanted to
know. He gave quizzes at the table. You knew your stuff or you
didn't get dessert, the best part of the meal.

I used to eat dinner in my friends' homes. I discovered that while no one's family is "normal"—at least not TV normal—each is normal in its own way. Reid's mom was from the South and always cooked up great southern dishes. His family loved sports, so we talked baseball, football, and basketball at the table. At Robert's house, the food was international—spicy and wonderful—and the conversation concentrated on politics and world affairs. Some moms insisted that we sit up straight, keep our elbows off the table, pass our food carefully, and ask permission to leave the table. At my house, the only rule was: Don't stab your brother with your fork.

Every family eats dinner, but each family eats dinner in its own way. Every family has its own "rules of the table," its own stories, its own inside jokes, and its own way of doing things. Similarly, each family has its own way of celebrating birthdays, tucking kids into bed at night, and taking family trips and vacations.

Which way is right? Which is "normal?" Is there one right way to eat dinner? Of course not. It's fascinating to experience all the differences, just as it's great to invite friends to enjoy my family's crazy dinner table, even today.

Religions are like families. Each religion has its own stories, its own ways of celebrating special days, and its own ways of talking to God. Each religion remembers the time when it felt closest to God: Jews remember the Exodus from Egypt, Christians remember the life of Jesus, and Muslims remember their prophet, Muhammed. By telling our religion's special story, we feel closer to the family of our religion and we feel closer to God. Each religion has its own rituals and symbols for celebrating the special moments of life and the cycle of each year. Each religion has its own ideas about what happens to people after they die, and each has its own ways of responding to the death of a loved one.

Religions also differ in the ideas they teach. Each religion has its own ideas about what makes life worth living, what our job is as human beings, what God is like, and why bad things happen to people. It's worth studying different religions to learn how people across the world and through history have answered these big questions about life. You will discover ideas in other religions that are powerful and interesting. You will discover how your own religion shares some ideas with other religions, and how it offers its own special ways of answering the big questions.

Just as there is not just one right way to "do" dinner, there's no one right way to do religion. But that doesn't make dinner or religion interchangeable any more than our families are interchangeable. I like visiting your home for dinner. Your mom may even be a better cook than mine. But my home is where I belong. In my home, my family shares our special family memories. We tell our family stories and enjoy the things we love to eat. In my religion, we share common memories, stories, and ways of celebrating. I belong to my religion just as I belong to my family.

Some people think the world would be a better place if we did away with all the differences and created one world religion. But that would be like getting rid of all the differences among our families. It would make us all into one, big, bland TV family. It's not only impossible to do away with our differences; it would take away an important part of who we are as human beings.

There isn't just one right way to do dinner, and there isn't one right way to do religion. But there are wrong ways. There are families where the table is a battleground— where dinnertime talk is hurtful, abusive, mean, and destructive. There are families where the food isn't shared, so some leave the table full while others leave hungry. There are wrong ways to do dinner, and there are wrong ways to do religion. Religions that teach hate are wrong. Religions that destroy human lives and disrespect human rights are wrong. My mom was right. In religion, just as in table manners, there is one basic rule: "Don't stab your brother with a fork."

WHAT IS CHRISTIAN RELIGION ABOUT? IS IT REALLY THAT DIFFERENT FROM OUR RELIGION?

Michelle told us more about the church service she attended.
"What is Christian religion about, anyway?" asked Josh.
"Is it really that different from our religion?"

Christianity is one of the world's great religions. It has many wise answers for the big questions of life. We live in a country where the vast majority of people are Christian. These are all important reasons why you should take the time to learn about Christianity.

Christianity is a very deep, very old, and very powerful faith. There are many versions of Christian belief and practice. It is very difficult to summarize such a deep tradition in a few moments. But just to get you started, here's a brief description.

Christianity is based on the life and teaching of Jesus, a Jew who lived in Israel during the first century, about two thousand years ago. The story of Jesus is contained in a book Christians call the New Testament, which is part of the Christian Bible. (Our Torah and Prophets are also parts of the Bible Christians use.) Jesus taught a way of coming close to God. He taught this to the Jews of his time. Later, after his death, his followers brought this teaching to those who weren't Jewish. They called it "good news," or "gospel," because it promised that God loves us human beings. Even when we make mistakes, Jesus taught, God still loves us.

After Jesus had become a well-known teacher in the north of Israel, in about the year 30 C.E. (after the year 0) he came to Jerusalem on Passover. In those days, Jews from all over the world made a pilgrimage to celebrate Passover in Jerusalem. This made it the best place to go if you wanted to spread a new religious message. Jerusalem, at that time, was governed by the Romans. The gathering of thousands of Jewish tourists made the Romans, who worried about a possible Jewish revolt, very nervous. As soon as Jesus began preaching his message, he was arrested by the Roman police, tried as a rebel, and executed publicly in a terrifying way—he was hung on a cross until he died. This was the standard way Romans executed criminals, particularly when they wanted to make a public example of someone. Jesus died late on a Friday. Since he couldn't be buried on the Sabbath, his followers placed his body in a tomb. According to the Christian story, when his followers came on Sunday to prepare the body for burial, it was gone. This is viewed as the most important event, known as the resurrection, in the Christian story. According to the story, Jesus later appeared to many of his followers, speaking with them, teaching them, and reassuring them.

Jews can read the stories of Jesus and believe that he was a great teacher. We can appreciate his message and compare it with the message of other Jewish teachers of the time; for example, Hillel. But Christians believe that Jesus was more than a person, more than a great teacher, even more than a prophet. For Christians, this story of returning after death proves that Jesus was much more than human. Christianity teaches that Jesus was a part of God.

The basic Christian idea is that human beings lie, cheat, steal, get angry, hurt one another, and perform endless other evils. That's our human nature. As a result, it is impossible for human beings to get close to God because God is perfect. This gap between human nature and God's perfection is what Christians call "sin." Many times, Christianity teaches, God offered us ways to heal this gap. But human beings failed. Finally, God offered an ultimate solution to the problem of sin. God sent part of Himself— or to put it in another way God sent His son—into the world to live as a human being and die on the cross. Jesus' death was a sacrifice that broke the power of sin in the world.

For Christians, Jesus unites God with human beings. Jesus is an example of how a person can live a Godly life. Jesus' death on the cross is a great act of loving self-sacrifice that can cleanse human beings of their sin and enable them to live more in harmony with God. The reward for cleansing oneself of evil and coming close to God is eternal life after death. This reward of life after death is what a Christian means by "being saved." This opportunity to conquer death is the great message of the Easter holiday.

The word "Christ" is the Greek translation of the Hebrew word *"mashiah"* or messiah. Literally, messiah means "anointed," from the ancient custom that a leader was crowned by pouring olive oil on his head. The Jewish idea began with the simple hope that one day God would send a leader to save the Jews from nations who oppressed them. Eventually, the idea grew to envision a leader who would bring peace to the whole world. The followers of Jesus believed that he was this special, chosen leader, and so they called him the Messiah, or the Christ. Jews, who respect Christianity and their Christian neighbors, call him by his name, Jesus, without the title, Christ.

Occasionally, I am invited to visit a church to teach about Judaism. They always ask the same question: "Why did the Jews reject Jesus Christ?" The truth is that we never rejected Jesus. We just have different ideas about God and human beings. Jews know as well as Christians that human beings do evil. But we don't believe this comes from human nature. Judaism believes that human beings *choose* between doing good and doing evil. When we choose evil, we sin, and we distance ourselves from God. For Christianity, sin is something we *are*. For Judaism, sin is something we *do*. Judaism does not believe in a permanent gap between God and us. We believe that whenever we choose evil, we can undo the damage. This is the Jewish idea of *Teshuva*, which means "turning" or "changing." Judaism teaches that we can always transform ourselves and bring ourselves back into harmony with God. To help us, God has given us the Torah and its commandments as a way of living a Godly life. This is the great message of the Yom Kippur holiday.

There is much that Judaism and Christianity share. We believe in one God. We believe that all people are created in God's image and are precious. We share the teachings of the Ten Commandments and many other lessons of the Bible. But we are different religions with different ideas and different ways of celebrating life.

CAN A PERSON BE HALF-JEWISH, HALF-CHRISTIAN?

"I have a friend who says he's half-Jewish, half-Christian,"
shares Ashley.

"I met a guy who said he was a Jew for Jesus," Josh
adds. "Is there such a thing?"

There are people who have one Jewish parent and one
Christian parent. There are families that celebrate the holidays of both religions in their home. Living in two religions
can be very difficult because a religion is more than just
holiday celebrations. Christianity and Judaism often teach
different things. Either you believe in Jesus, or you believe
in *Teshuva*. Either you celebrate Easter, or you celebrate
Yom Kippur. If you walk into a church, usually the first thing
you see in front of you is the cross. For Christians, the cross
is the greatest symbol of God's love. Through the cross,
which symbolizes for Christians the life, teaching, death,
and resurrection of Jesus, Christians come close to God. In
a synagogue, the first thing you see is the ark holding the
scrolls of the Torah. The Torah is the Jews' symbol of God's
love. Through the Torah, its commandments and teachings,
Jews come close to God. Being a Christian is very admirable
and beautiful. Being a Jew is equally admirable and beautiful. But being a "Jew for Jesus" combines things that are
impossible to mix.

We should study other religions. We should learn

about our similarities and differences. We should respect each other. But combining religions doesn't give you a new one that's better. Ketchup is good. And ice cream is good. Mix them and what you get isn't necessarily better.

WHY WON'T MOM LET US HAVE A CHRISTMAS TREE?

"All right, I know we're Jewish," concedes Ashley, "but why won't my mom let us have a Christmas tree? Everyone else has one. It's really not a religious thing anymore. What's so wrong with it?"

When I was young, my brothers and I cornered my mom, and we demanded a Christmas tree. We were the only ones on the block without one. They're so beautiful. And besides, we argued, Christmas isn't a religious holiday anymore. It's just a shopping holiday! So why can't we have a tree with presents like all the other kids in school?!

Mom listened carefully, nodded her head, and said, "OK. You can have a tree."

We were shocked. We never expected her to agree. "Really?"

She nodded her head, "Sure."

"With lights and tinsel and a star on top?" my little brother asked.

"Of course, all of it," said Mom, "… in July."

A Christmas tree is a beautiful symbol. And if you put one up in July, it's not religious. In July, it's just a decoration. But in December, it has another meaning. In December, it is the sacred symbol of another religion. For religious Christians, the Christmas tree has deep meaning. It represents the birth of Christ. It is an evergreen tree and stands for the gift of life everlasting through Christ. The presents beneath the tree represent the gifts the magi, the wise men, brought to the Christ child on the night of his birth. The lights of the tree represent the light of God's love reflected in the Christ child.

What does it mean to bring the symbol of another religion into our home? What does it say to our Christian neighbors? What does it say about us?

A few years ago, there was a Paris fashion designer who took Jewish religious objects and used them for fashion accessories. *Vogue*, the world's most important fashion magazine, showed pictures of beautiful models wearing a tallit over a mini-skirt, tefillin as a kind of jewelry, and a *kippah* as a hat. How does that feel to Jews? How would we feel if a Christian family brought a Torah scroll into their home as a decoration, like a piece of art? Christmas trees are pretty. And it's true that, for many Christians, this holiday has lost all its religious meaning. But there are many religious Christians in our communities who have a right to be outraged when people, especially non-Christians, use their holy symbol just because it's pretty and turn their holy day into a shopping holiday.

It's sad that people find so little in their own traditions that they need to take someone else's symbol and holiday. It's sad that they give up so much wisdom and history just to do what everyone else on the block does. It's sad that they haven't discovered the joy of being Jewish.

Our Christian neighbors have beautiful holidays. We have our own beautiful holidays. We can certainly visit our neighbors to share the beauty and joy of their holidays. We can invite them to our home to share our celebrations. We can learn about each others' holidays and the important ideas behind them. We can recognize our similarities and acknowledge our differences. These differences are important. There are billions of people on earth, but no two faces exactly alike. It would have been much simpler if God had made us all alike, but God loves differences—and so should we.

11

Why Do People Hate Jews?

HOW COME IN HISTORY EVERYONE'S OUT TO GET THE JEWS?

Jennifer finished The Diary of Anne Frank *and asked me for some more books about the Holocaust. One afternoon she asked me, "How come in history everyone's out to get the Jews? What did we do to deserve this?"*

There was a court case written up in the newspaper some time ago about a high school student, a boy of about sixteen, who attacked a female classmate in the stairwell of their school one afternoon after school. At the trial, the judge decided that the boy was not guilty because the girl was wearing a short, tight outfit. Wearing clothes like that in public, the judge reasoned, she was "asking for trouble," and the boy should not be held responsible.

This is called "blaming the victim." It's crazy and it's outrageous, but it happens sometimes.

When studying the history of Jewish persecution, many people commit the same crazy, outrageous mistake. Over the past two thousand years, Jews have been exiled from their homeland and have experienced hatred, discrimination, exclusion, murderous riots, forced conversion, and genocidal Holocaust. Millions of Jews have been murdered for the sole crime of being Jewish. Why? Many people believe it's the Jews' own fault. They'll say: Jews wouldn't have suffered persecution if they weren't so:

> Separate, cliquish, and different
>
> Eager to become just like us and join our society
>
> Pushy
>
> Passive
>
> Into money
>
> Into religion
>
> Cheap
>
> Charitable
>
> Nosey
>
> Standoffish
>
> Liberal
>
> Conservative
>
> Loud
>
> Quiet
>
> Sneaky
>
> In-your-face
>
> Jewish!

You name it; someone will blame Jews for it. There's even hatred for Jews in countries like Japan, where almost no Jews live. Sure, there are Jewish people that have some of these characteristics. But there are plenty of other people like this as well. Giving these as the reasons for persecution is a great example of blaming the victim. Jews suffer so much, the reasoning goes, that they must be doing something to bring it on themselves. Just like that girl in the high school was "asking for trouble" walking down the stairwell, minding her own business. Crazy! Outrageous!

The truth is that Jews have suffered for thousands of years not because anything they did was wrong, but because of the wrong thinking and evil behavior of those who persecuted them. Hate, anger, intolerance, small-mindedness, arrogance, evil—these are the reasons Jews have been made to suffer.

Scholars have studied the history of anti-Semitism (the word for hating Jews) and have taught many theories for why it happens:

- Some say that the reason lies in religion. The Christian religion taught that the Jews rejected Jesus and needed to suffer for that sin. The Church used to use the Jews as an example to show what happens when people turn away from their religion.
- Others see it in economic terms. Jews were forbidden by the rules of Christian Europe from owning land or entering craft guilds. So they entered other

professions, including money-lending, which was forbidden to Christians. Christians often found themselves owing a great deal of money to the Jews. Hatred soon followed. (Who likes the guy you owe money to?) If Jews were murdered in a riot, then the debts were erased.

- Still others understand anti-Semitism as a form of scapegoating. Times were hard, people were hungry, sometimes a plague would come, and many would die of disease. People looked to blame someone. The Jews had a different religion and different customs. They were a distinct community that didn't mix with everyone else. We fear those who are different. It was easy to blame the Jews for whatever went wrong.

There are scholars who point to the fact that even in the worst of times, Jews often lived better than their Christian neighbors. Because of the Jewish respect for education, Jews were almost always literate, while most Christians could not read or write. The Jewish community cared for their poor, for orphans and widows, so that, even in the worst of times, no one was left to starve. There was much less drunkenness, wife abuse, or child abuse in the Jewish community. Perhaps anti-Semitism was rooted in the envy others felt for the Jewish way of life.

We study this painful history of anti-Semitism to protect ourselves from future outbreaks of hatred and prejudice.

We study it also to protect ourselves from becoming like the people who hurt us. We want to make sure we don't fall into the traps of evil, hatred, and prejudice against others that led to the destruction of so many of our own people. The very worst response to our own suffering is to make others suffer. Because we remember being slaves in Egypt, we work tirelessly to make sure that no one anywhere suffers as we did. We've known hatred and suffering all through our history. It's our responsibility to bring an end to hatred and suffering everywhere.

12

If We Live Here, Why Is Israel So Important?

WHAT'S THE BIG DEAL WITH ISRAEL ANYWAY?

"This summer, my mom wants to take our family to Israel in honor of my Bat Mitzvah," Nicole shared with us, *"but I'd rather go to Hawaii. What's the big deal with Israel anyway? Aren't we* American Jews?*"*

Ever been away from home for a long time—on a long trip, or a summer at camp? Remember what it's like to come home? You turn the corner onto your street, and it feels special. It's not just any street, it's *your* street. Then you stop in front of your house. And it feels even more special. Then you go into your room, and you know you're home. All your stuff is there. Your memories of special times are there. It feels and smells like home. You know that you belong there. That's how the Jewish people feel about Israel.

For almost two thousand years, we were exiled, forced to live far from home in lands ruled by others, often by those who hated us. Finally, in 1948, we were allowed to return home. Israel is the home of the Jewish people. It's where the most important events of our growing up as a people took place. It's the land God promised to our patriarchs and matriarchs in the Torah. It's the land of King David and King Solomon. It's the place where the prophets preached, where the Holy Temple stood, where the Maccabees fought.

Israel is a country whose purpose is to protect the Jewish people. When the Jews of Ethiopia were threatened in that country's civil war, Israel airlifted thousands to new lives in Israel. When the Soviet Union allowed Jews to leave, Israel welcomed thousands. Israel is the gathering place for Jews from around the world. Walk the streets and you'll meet Jews from Yemen, Morocco, Iraq, Norway, Argentina, and Canada.

In America, we live freely as Jews, but being Jewish is confined to our private lives—what we do at home or in synagogue. In Israel, the public life of a whole society is Jewish. The national language is Hebrew. Jewish holidays are national holidays. Shabbat is everyone's day off. This presents us with interesting new problems never before faced in Jewish history. For example, what's it like to be a Jewish army? What are the Jewish rules for making war and seeking peace? What does the Jewish tradition teach us about protecting the environment? Is there a Jewish way to pick up and dispose of trash? Is there a Jewish way to run a government, to educate children, to care for the elderly? In Israel, we get to find a Jewish way to do everything, and everything becomes a Jewish question.

Do you know how Israel got its flag? The First Zionist Congress met in Basel, a small city in Switzerland, in 1897, beginning the process that would lead to the establishment of the Jewish state. Theodor Herzl, the man whose dream set in motion this historic process, asked his aide, David Wolffsohn, to find a flag for the meeting room. After all, if we were going to have a country, we needed a flag. But what would be a Jewish flag? Jews had not had a country of their own for almost two thousand years, and they had never had a flag.

A stranger to Basel, Wolffsohn had no idea where to go to find a flag. And he had only an hour! He ran through the boulevards of the city, scouring the shops, but found nothing appropriate. Exhausted and frustrated, he entered a small synagogue to rest a moment. There he saw his flag. He took a large blue and white tallit, removed the fringes, and with a fountain pen, inscribed a Magen David in the center. That's how Israel's flag was born.

Israel is a country whose flag is really a tallit. It is a place where every part of life can be Jewish. It is the fulfillment of the dreams and prayers of so many generations of the Jewish people.

Are You Sure We Should Go?

"But I heard it's really dangerous in Israel, that they're always fighting," Nicole worried. "Are you sure we should go?"

Since its very beginning, in 1948, Israel has been at war with its Arab neighbors. Jews feel we have a right to return our homeland in Israel. There have always been communities of Jews living in Israel, sometimes outnumbering the Arabs there. And Israel has always been at the center of our religious life, no matter where we lived. Our right to Israel was confirmed when the United Nations voted to establish the State of Israel in November 1947.

The Arab countries that surround Israel and the Palestinian Arabs who live on the West Bank and in the Gaza Strip never accepted our right. They believe that Jews came to an Arab land and stole it. They have fought Israel's existence from its very beginning.

During this time, there have been signs that peace is not impossible. In 1977, Anwar Sadat, president of Egypt, flew to Jerusalem to make peace with Israel. In 1994, King Hussein of Jordan signed a peace agreement with Israel as well. The original United Nations plan proposed splitting the land between a Jewish State of Israel and a Palestinian Arab state. In recent years, Israel and its neighbors have struggled to find a way to carry out this plan—giving Palestinian Arabs their own state in return for peace with

Israel. The struggle has often been painful and bloodied by war and terrorism. But we have not lost hope that peace will come, as an Israeli folk song goes; if not tomorrow, then surely the day after.

The amazing thing about Israel is that, even in the worst of times, it is a place full of life, energy, and hope. It's an exciting place filled with history and beauty. Every place in Israel, every street corner, every neighborhood, every hilltop and valley, tells a special story. Here's where Elijah stood, and there's where Rabbi Akiba taught. Here's Hillel's house, and there Yitzchak Rabin lived. There are beautiful beaches, great shopping, and warm people. At the end of your trip, you'll feel such a special sense of belonging, you won't want to leave. That's why we call it our homeland.

You need to go to Israel to really understand how special it is. You need to experience Israel for yourself to know that it's your homeland. It may be more dangerous than going to Hawaii, but a week after Hawaii, all you'll have is a sunburn. A visit to Israel will give you a new idea of who you are.

13

Orthodox, Conservative, Reconstructionist, Reform—Why Can't I Just Be Jewish?

"I have a cousin who is Orthodox," Jason related. "We visited him last Sunday. He's verrrry religious. But I don't understand all this. What's Orthodox? What's Conservative? What's Reform? Can't I just be Jewish?"

According to the story in the Torah, when the people of Israel left Egypt, they journeyed through the desert for forty years. During that time, God fed them something called "manna." The Torah doesn't tell us too much about manna. Later, scholars wondered what it tasted like. Manna, they imagined, tasted like whatever each person wanted it to taste like. For a baby, it was like sweet milk; for a kid, like candy; for an adult, like a satisfying meal. It was the same stuff, but it tasted different to each person. Miracle food!

When these same Israelites arrived at Mount Sinai, according to the Torah, God spoke to them. Again, scholars wondered, what did God's voice sound like? They offered a similar answer. They all heard the voice of God, but each person heard the voice that he or she needed to hear. Some heard a soft, gentle voice. Some heard a powerful, commanding voice. Miracle voice!

There have always been different ways to be Jewish—different ways for Jewish people to experience God and to celebrate their being Jewish. Two thousand years ago, there were groups called Sadducees and Pharasees, each teaching their own way to be Jewish. The Talmud is filled with arguments and disagreements among rabbis and scholars on the meaning of the Torah and what God expects of us. Sometimes our differences have turned extreme. When the great scholar Maimonides wrote his book of Jewish ideas, other rabbis disagreed with him so much, they burned it!

There have always been different ways to be Jewish. Some people find this terribly frustrating. They believe that differences are a weakness and we should unite around one uniform set of beliefs and practices. The question is, whose beliefs and practices? And beyond that, what happens to those of us who don't fit in? If there were only one way to be Jewish, only one way to know God and celebrate Jewish life, those of us who disagreed or differed would have to leave. Imagine going into a restaurant where the menu had only one thing on it—especially if that's something you don't like. Frustrating as it might be, it's the differences among us that have actually enabled the Jewish people to stay together as a people and as a religion these past thousands of years.

In our time, we have four major "movements" of Judaism: Orthodox, Conservative, Reform, and Reconstructionist. All these movements include serious Jews who live faithfully according to the Jewish tradition. Orthodox Jews aren't "more Jewish" or "more religious" than Reform Jews. What separates these movements are their answers to this question: What is expected of us as Jews? And don't think that the disagreements are only between the movements. Within each movement, there is plenty of debate, disagreement, and even conflict.

Orthodox Judaism teaches that the Torah and all its traditions were given us by God. God expects us to obey these laws and traditions. The word "Orthodox" means "according to the law." There are many different kinds of Orthodox Jews, depending on how they balance living by the tradition's laws and being part of our world. I have Orthodox friends, for example, who don't own a television, never see movies, and never read books or magazines from outside their Orthodox community. They dress much more modestly than we do and try to have as little to do with the "outside world" as possible. My other Orthodox friends dress and act just as I do. They participate in every part of modern life, while carefully keeping the laws and traditions of the Jewish people. They are big baseball fans. They go to the ballpark, but they bring their own kosher food. My friend wears a baseball cap, and underneath it he wears a black *kippah*. What makes them all Orthodox is their belief that by keeping God's law, every bit of life becomes an expression of closeness to God.

Conservative Judaism also believes that the laws and traditions come from God. But Conservative Judaism believes that God gave these laws to human beings and gave human beings the important job of interpreting, adjusting, and changing the laws and traditions in each generation. The meaning of "Conservative" is the same as "conserving"—protecting and keeping something safe. We conserve God's law by making sure it fits the times and the needs of each generation.

One of the most important changes Conservative Judaism brought to Jewish law and tradition has to do with what women do in the synagogue. For most of Jewish history, women were not permitted to be synagogue leaders, rabbis, or cantors. Conservative rabbis studied this carefully and decided excluding women wasn't right, that it was immoral to exclude people because of their gender and impractical to limit those who could serve as rabbis and cantors, excluding half of the population. Women have the same level of capacity as men to serve as leaders, teachers, and interpreters of the tradition's wisdom, they decided, so they changed the law. And now there are women who serve as rabbis, cantors, and leaders in almost every Conservative synagogue. What makes them Conservative is their belief that God expects us to "grow" the laws and traditions in order to keep them alive and strong.

Reform Judaism believes that every Jew must find his or her own way to experience God and celebrate being Jewish. The traditions and customs of Jewish practice are like a giant library that Jews can choose from to come close to God and the Jewish people. Reform Judaism believes that there are commandments when it comes to Jewish ethics. But unlike Orthodox and Conservative Judaism, Reform Judaism believes there is no "law" that governs Jewish ritual life. One's ritual life is a matter of individual choice as one decides how to come close to God.

Because Reform Judaism is not bound by ritual law, the Reform Movement was the first to change the way women participate in synagogue life. The Reform Movement was the first to ordain women as rabbis and cantors.

According to Reform Judaism, Jews choose what makes sense to them; therefore, Judaism will naturally change from generation to generation. This is the meaning of "Reform"—a tradition that is always in a process of growth and change. Reform Judaism believes that this choice must be an intelligent choice, so Reform Judaism demands that Jews carefully study Jewish teachings and practices as they make their choices.

A central idea in Reform Judaism is the Jewish responsibility to do *tikkun olam*, to be God's partner in repairing the world. Reform Judaism has always been very active in programs to help the poor and the homeless—not only because it's the right thing to do, but as a way of being Jewish, a way of coming close to God.

Reconstructionist Judaism was created by a great American Jewish thinker, Mordecai M. Kaplan. Kaplan believed that religion is the creation of a human community as it imagined how the world ought to be. The first and most important truth about being Jewish, taught Kaplan, is belonging to the Jewish people and sharing its life. Judaism, he taught, wasn't just religion, but all the things Jews do to express their connection with the Jewish people, including literature, music, art, cooking, politics, and so forth. Judaism, Kaplan taught, is a "civilization." And because the Jewish people are always changing, Judaism is always changing.

If you look around your synagogue, even if it's not Reconstructionist, you can see the impact of Mordecai M. Kaplan. When your grandparents were your age, the synagogue was basically a place where people prayed. Occasionally, the synagogue would also be a classroom or a place for a wedding, but primarily, it was a place of prayer. Look at all the things that go on in a synagogue today: dance classes, lectures on family life, programs of Jewish music, nursery school for tots, support groups for mourners, youth groups for teens, groups for older people, groups for couples, groups for singles. Why does this happen in the synagogue? What has it all to do with Judaism? It was Mordecai Kaplan's idea that Judaism is more than just religion. Judaism is all that brings Jews together, and the synagogue should be the place for it all.

Have you ever heard an orchestra playing a piece of

music? As you listen, you realize that the musicians aren't playing the same thing. What makes orchestra music interesting is that each instrument, each musician, is playing something different. And yet, it all combines into one magnificent sound. Perhaps that's what God hears when we all practice Judaism in our different ways. To us, it sounds like conflicts and contradictions. But God hears the harmonies and the melodies and enjoys the music.

 *14*

What Happens to Us After We Die?

DO JEWS BELIEVE IN HEAVEN AND HELL?

"We went back to visit my aunt's family ... you know, the one who was sick. She died last week and they're so very sad," Molly told me one afternoon before class. "So I was wondering if you could tell me, what happens to people after they die? Do Jews believe in heaven and hell?"

If you ask most Americans, you'll find that the question of life after death is the number-one question most people ask of their religion. If you go to the library and check out a book on world religions, you will find that this question is at the very top of the list of important religious questions. It's curious, there-fore, that so little attention is given to this question in Jewish life. Visit a church three weeks in a row, and you'll hear two ser-mons about how we earn life after death. Visit a synagogue for an entire year, and maybe you will hear one mention of heaven, hell, or life after death. Even the Bible doesn't seem to be concerned with the question. In the entire story of Abraham, only four verses tell about his death. Only four verses describe the death of Moses. And there is nothing about their getting into heaven, or anything connected with their life after death.

Life after death is not as important to Judaism as life before death. Life in the "next world" is not as important as life in this world.

Many people use their belief in life after death as a way of escaping concern and responsibility for the condition of this world. After all, they tell themselves, if my life in this world is only temporary and if my life in the "next world" is so much better, why care? Why bother with all the problems here and now? Judaism refuses to let us escape from our responsibility in this world. You and I are God's partners, and we have much to do! The philosopher Abraham Joshua Heschel once remarked, "We Jews believe in another world. We just take our worlds one at a time."

Some religions use their belief in life after death as a way of scaring people: "Believe our way, or else!" Some religious groups offer very detailed descriptions of all sorts of terrible things that await those who refuse to accept their way of doing religion. Judaism believes in a God who created everyone and loves everyone. If there's heaven, you don't have to be Jewish to get there. You have to be a person who has accepted the responsibility of being God's partner. We believe that good people of all religions have a place in the "next world." We've talked about Raul Wallenberg and Sempo Sugihara. Wouldn't you think that God has a special place in heaven for righteous people like them?

Our thinking about afterlife begins with a question about what it means to be human: Am I just a body? If I'm only a body, when my body dies, I die—I'm gone, and nothing lives on. Perhaps there is some part of us which is not body, not physical, so that when we die, this part goes on living. We've talked about having a "self." Others call this part of us the "soul" or "spirit." The truth is, like the words "God" and "self," the words "soul" and "spirit" have no easy definition. If I have a soul—or if I am a soul—what's the soul made of? Where does it go when a person dies?

People believe in the soul because of an intuition or a feeling we have that there's more to us than our physical body. We sense that the body is a container, a vessel, for something precious. When my children were born, I had this powerful feeling that there was a whole world of personality packed into that tiny package. When my grandfather died, it was hard to believe that all his wisdom and humor and experience were contained in that very fragile, very delicate container. He was so strong, but his body so weak. He was so big, but his body so small. He was so full of life one moment, and so empty the next.

As with many questions of belief, there isn't just one, but many different Jewish opinions on this question for you to try on:

- There have been Jewish thinkers who believed that we live our lives in this world, and when we die, we die. We live on, in a way, through our families, through the people who remember us, and through all the things we did to make a change in this world.
- Other thinkers proposed that the human being has a soul as well as a body. When we die, our soul returns to God like the wave returning to the ocean.
- Some thinkers have believed that, after death, the soul is judged—rewarded for all the good it did in the world, and punished for all the evil it did. Some have described in very detailed and colorful terms what heaven and hell might be like.
- There are Jewish thinkers who believe that souls are reborn in new bodies and start life all over again. Others believe that souls are stored up with God until a special day comes when all will be reborn—resurrected—to live again, perhaps to live forever in a world without death.

All of these are Jewish beliefs offered by great Jewish thinkers at different times in Jewish history. What they have in common is a belief in a God who loves us, who created us, and who will care for us when we die.

The beliefs in heaven and hell—a life after this one—come from our sadness and anger at all the unfairness in the world. How can we make sense of the contradiction between people's goodness and the terrible things that happen to them in this life? Is it possible that 6 million Jews were murdered in the Holocaust—their lives stolen from them—and that there is no punishment for those who murdered them? Is it possible that those innocent Jewish victims and the criminals who brought so much pain and destruction are in the same place?

This is a very old question. The Talmud tells a sad story:

> A boy was ordered by his father to climb to the top of a tall tree and collect some small birds from a nest. The boy obeyed his father, which fulfilled a commandment of the Torah, "Honor your father and your mother" (Exodus 20:12), and climbed to the treetop. Just before taking the baby birds, the boy shooed away the mother bird. In so doing, he fulfilled another commandment of the Torah, "Do not take the mother together with her young, but let the mother go and take only the young" (Deuteronomy 22:6–7). On the way down the ladder, the boy fell and died. The Rabbis who witnessed this event were heartbroken. The death of any young person is terrible. But here the boy was in the very process of fulfilling two commandments of the Torah. And more, these are two special commandments—the Torah promises the

reward of a long and good life for fulfillment of these two commandments. The Rabbis concluded that only way to make sense of the world's unfairness—to resolve the contradiction between the Torah's promise and the events of the world—is to conclude that there is another world, a world of true justice, *olam ha-ba*, a world to come (*Kiddushin* 39a).

The real question isn't what happens after we die. After all, no one alive knows. We trust that the same God who loves us and gave us life will care for us when we die. The real question is, what do we do until then? How do we live? And if we are concerned about death, we might ask, what can death teach us about living? One thing I've learned is to remember that, as much as we want to live a long, long time, no one has an endless number of tomorrows. If we need to say "thank you," "I love you," or "I'm sorry" to someone, we need to say it today. If there is someone whose friendship we desire, go make friends today. If we have dreams to pursue, projects to do, goals to achieve, we need to begin today. The Bible's Book of Psalms offers a very powerful prayer: "Teach us to number our days that we may have a wise heart" (Psalms 90:12). Knowing about death may help us to appreciate the gift of life and to live fully each day.

15

What's the Messiah?

Ricky came in with a pile of bumper stickers. "My Orthodox cousin gave me these cool Jewish bumper stickers for everyone. They say, 'We want Mashiah now!' When I asked him what it meant, he said it was our prayer for the Messiah. What's the Messiah? And why does my cousin want the Messiah so much?"

Did you ever dream about what the world would be like if it were perfect? No war, violence, hunger, or disease; no pollution, deceit, or hatred.

This kind of dreaming is an old hobby of the Jewish people. Maybe because we've been the victim of so much persecution. Maybe because we've always been a small, weak people getting beat up by everyone bigger. Maybe because we believe in a God who is God of everyone and everything. We've always had great dreams about a better world.

One of the greatest of these Jewish dreamers was a prophet named Isaiah who lived in about 740 B.C.E. (before the year 0). He worried about the future of his beloved city, Jerusalem. Great empires were sweeping the world, destroying everything in their path. He dreamed about a day when Jerusalem would be the world capitol of peace, when the whole world would come together and be one. Here are his words:

> In the days to come,
> The Mount of the LORD's House
> Shall stand firm above the mountains
> And tower above the hills;
> And all the nations
> Shall gaze on it with joy.
> And the many peoples shall go and say:
> "Come,
> Let us go up to the Mount of the LORD,
> To the House of the God of Jacob;
> That He may instruct us in His ways,
> And that we may walk in His paths."
> For Torah [teaching] shall come forth
>   from Zion,
> The word of the LORD from Jerusalem.
> Thus He will judge among the nations
> And make peace for the many peoples,
> And they shall beat their swords into
>   plowshares

And their spears into pruning hooks:
Nation shall not take up
Sword against nation;
They shall never again know war.
—Isaiah 2:2–4 (Translation from *Tanakh*.
Philadelphia: Jewish Publication Society, 1985)

Isaiah imagined a world without war. He imagined a world where everyone would come to Jerusalem to settle their differences and listen to God's wisdom. The world would be so peaceful, people would turn their weapons into farm tools and grow food.

About 150 years after Isaiah, the city of Jerusalem was destroyed and its people sent into exile, just as he had worried. The Jewish people put all their hopes together into one dream: They dreamed of returning to Jerusalem and rebuilding the city. They dreamed of crowning a new king as great as King David. And they continued Isaiah's dream of a world of peace.

As I mentioned before, in ancient times, when a person became king, they poured olive oil on his head. A person crowned with oil in this way is called in English "anointed"; in Hebrew, "*mashiach*." This is where we get the word "messiah."

As we discussed earlier, originally the Messiah was to be the new king who would rule over the new, rebuilt Jerusalem. Soon the dream got bigger. The Israelites dreamed of a messiah who wasn't just a king, but a messenger of God who would bring to life all their dreams—of a world of peace, love, and blessings. Some day, Jews told one another, the Messiah will come and make the world perfect. But when?

The Rabbis of the Talmud taught:

If you are planting a tree and someone comes along shouting, "The Messiah is here! The Messiah is here!" finish planting the tree. Then go see if it's true (A*vot* d'R*abbi* N*atan*).

It's wonderful to dream. Our dreams give us hope and they tell us what to strive for, what to work for. But dreaming must never get in the way of the important things we have to do in the world. Let's work hard to make the world peaceful and whole. Let's find a way to end war, hatred, and violence; to end hunger, disease, and need. Then, if the Messiah comes, great! And if not, well, if we're successful, we won't need a messiah. So, first plant your tree, and then go see.

16

What's a Bar Mitzvah? What's a Bat Mitzvah? Can't I Just Have a Birthday Party?

Mitchell was a very serious student. He was working hard getting ready for his Bar Mitzvah. The pressure and expectations were getting to him. He came into class one afternoon ready to give it all up.

"Who needs this?" he screamed at me.

"It's your Bar Mitzvah, aren't you excited?" I asked. That was probably the wrong thing to say.

Mitchell sat glum for a few minutes. When he calmed down, he asked me, "Why am I getting Bar Mitzvah'ed? What's a Bar/Bat Mitzvah anyway? Why can't I just have a party?"

Let's get the language straight. In Jewish tradition, you don't "have a Bar/Bat Mitzvah" and you don't get "Bar Mitzvah'ed." You *become* a Bat Mitzvah or a Bar Mitzvah. And that language is very important. This is about becoming something. You're at a time in your life when important changes are happening to you and in you. You're no longer the little kid you were just a few years ago. Now you're reaching toward adulthood. The important question is, what does it mean to be an adult? How do you get there?

Most cultures have some symbolic ritual recognizing a child's transition into adulthood. These rites reflect the most important values of that culture. Among the tribes of the Australian aborigines, for example, a boy is forcibly kidnapped from his mother's tent by masked warriors sometime between his twelfth and sixteenth birthdays. He is taken to a secret holy place in the wilderness where the tribe's leaders beat him and try to scare him almost to death as they attempt to root out the child-spirit that's in him. If he survives, the boy is taught the ways of the tribe's adult men. As a final sign of maturity, the tribe's elders knock out one of his teeth. He then returns to the tribe to live—not with his family, but among the other hunters and warriors.

Still think Bar Mitzvah is scary?

In American culture, becoming an adult means permission to do new things: drive, drink alcohol, get into R-rated movies, and vote in elections. No wonder kids can't wait to grow up! What kids don't see are the responsibilities that come along with these privileges. In America, we celebrate only the freedoms of adulthood and not the responsibilities that come with them. Driving means getting around where and when you want. But it's a huge responsibility to drive safely and responsibly. Every day people die on our roads and freeways because of someone else's carelessness.

In Jewish life, becoming an adult is not about scaring you and it's not about new privileges. Being an adult means being responsible. It means that your family, your community, and God can count on you. We count on you to do your part in helping us to fix all the broken parts of the world—hunger, disease, hurt, war. We count on you to help bring the world close to God's dream. That's hard work. But it feels special knowing that people count on you. It feels special knowing that you're important enough that people expect something from you.

The phrases "Bar Mitzvah" for boys and "Bat Mitzvah" for girls means one who is responsible—someone we can count on—which is the most important part of being a Jewish adult. For a Jew, the sign of becoming an adult is the ability to understand the Torah and to teach it to other adults. The Torah is the story of how our people accepted the responsibility of sharing God's dreams for the world. To have a Bar/Bat Mitzvah, you don't really need the party, the DJ, or the presents. All you need is a community of adults who have gathered to learn the Torah, and a young person who is ready to step up and say, "I'm ready to be responsible." That young person is called to the Torah—not just to hear the Torah, but to share in teaching it to others.

In the Jewish community, boys have been celebrating their becoming Bar Mitzvah since the time of the Talmud. For girls, the first public Bat Mitzvah where a girl was invited to read from the Torah took place only in 1922, when Rabbi Mordecai M. Kaplan, the founder of Reconstructionism, celebrated his daughter Judith's growing up.

All this may sound difficult. You're not a rabbi, so how are you supposed to teach Torah to others? Don't worry. The Bar/Bat Mitzvah ceremony doesn't mean that you're finished growing up or that you're now an adult or that you know everything. It really means that you've begun the *process* of growing up. You've started on the pathway to becoming an adult. Most people start on that pathway when they begin their teen years, so the Jewish tradition decided to just set an age for Bar/Bat Mitzvah—thirteen for boys and, because girls generally grow a little faster than boys at this age, between twelve and thirteen for girls. Some people will be more mature than others at this age. But everyone is given the chance to celebrate the beginning of this amazing passage from being a kid to becoming an adult.

WHY DO WE HAVE TO KEEP GOING TO HEBREW SCHOOL EVEN AFTER WE'RE BAR MITZVAH?

As we began talking about Bar and Bat Mitzvah getting closer, I talked to the class about what they'd be doing next year. I told them that I hoped they would continue coming to the high school program in the Hebrew School. This came as a shock. It was Josh who expressed the thoughts of his classmates,

"Are you nuts? We'll be Bar Mitzvah!" he shouted. "That means we're done with Hebrew School!"

"You won't be done," I explained. "You're just getting started."

"But we're teenagers now; why do we have to keep going to Hebrew School even after we're Bar Mitzvah?"

Why do you go to regular school? Why bother with high school, let alone college? You're a teen now—a young adult. You've probably been in school since you were two or three years old. You know how to read and do basic math. You know a few dates in American history. What else do you need to know? What can they teach you that you don't already know?

The answer, of course, is that there is a whole world of knowledge and wisdom that your early years in school have only prepared you to discover. The best is yet to come.

Unlike animals, we human beings are born with very few instincts. The collective wisdom of, say, dogs is transmitted through the genes as instinct. That is, dogs are born knowing everything they need to know about being a dog. In contrast, humans share their wisdom through culture—through literature, art, and science. That's what you have to look forward to in high school and beyond: joining the great human conversation; debating ideas with Socrates, Shakespeare, Einstein, and Freud; soaring the heavens with

Beethoven and Van Gogh; peering deeply into human life through the eyes of Charles Dickens and Herman Melville.

Jewish culture is no different. Jewish culture is the collective wisdom of our civilization, passed to you in literature, symbols, and custom. We call this conversation Torah. Study Torah and you are invited to join one of the world's longest and deepest ongoing conversations about being human. Open the Bible. Open the Talmud. Open the prayer book. Open a book of Yiddish stories or of Ladino poetry. Immediately you find yourself at the table listening in on the greatest Jewish minds: Rabbi Akiba of second-century Israel debating Rashi of eleventh-century France; Yehuda Halevi of fifteenth-century Spain sharing a good story with the Baal Shem Tov in eighteenth-century Poland; the prophet Jeremiah of Jerusalem in 600 B.C.E. complaining to the Rambam of twelfth-century Egypt. Like any Jewish family, they're all talking, arguing, and telling stories as they search together to find the way to come close to God, to bring wholeness to the world, to live a life that matters. Studying Torah is the way we get the tools and the plans for making the world whole. Here are the great masters, the artists of repairing the world, and they're ready to share their secrets with you.

The best is yet to come. Hebrew school has only given to you the beginnings, the basic tools. Now, you're almost ready to join the great conversation. And once you do, you're never finished. In Jewish life, you never finish learning—there's no such thing as "graduation." A Jewish scholar is called a *"Talmid Hacham"*—a wise student. It doesn't matter how old you are; you're always a student. You're always learning, growing, discovering. And if you're good at it, your opinions will be recorded. You'll become part of the eternal conversation. Generations and generations in the future, on Mars, Endor, Vulcan, or wherever Jews live centuries from now, Jews will learn your ideas and follow your wisdom.

There is a story of a poor farmer:

He tried for years and years to cultivate a field. But the field was filled with rocks. He toiled for years trying to clear the rocks from the field so he could grow a few potatoes for his family. Finally, he gave up and sold the field. He warned the new owner what a terrible field it was. The new owner came and inspected the field. Instead of throwing the rocks away, as had his predecessor, he picked them up to see what sort of rocks these were. He hit two of the rocks together and out fell a handful of diamonds. Indeed, this was a very poor field—for potatoes. But it turned out to be the richest diamond field in the world.

You're standing on a field filled with diamonds. But you'll find the field's riches only if you know what to look for—and only if you don't walk away.

17

Why Is It So Important to Marry Someone Jewish?

WHY CAN'T I JUST MARRY SOMEONE I LOVE?

Our discussion of everyone's becoming a Bar or Bat Mitzvah led to a conversation about being an adult. And that led to discussions about relationships.

"My mom says that when I get older, I have to marry someone Jewish. Why? Why can't I just marry someone I love?"

Suppose I love classical music. What would happen if I have an intimate relationship with someone who hates classical music but loves heavy-metal rock? I'm into symphonies, violin concertos, piano recitals. She's into head-banging mosh pits at painfully loud concerts filled with punk rockers. I collect Beethoven, Brahms, Bach. She collects Metallica, Megadeth, Nine-Inch Nails. But we're in love.

Living with such a person would mean a lot of changes. I couldn't play my favorite classical music CDs in the house. I wouldn't be able to take my partner to the concerts I enjoy. I couldn't share the thrill of finding a great new CD or of meeting my favorite musician. And she'd have to make the same changes. Such a relationship would mean that I would have to give up a great deal of myself. What kind of love is that? And how long could we be happy?

It is said: Love is blind. That's not true: Desire is blind. People can fall in love with others who are very different. We can have intense relationships with others whose values and interests and ideas and backgrounds are very different. But these relationships rarely last long. Eventually, we get tired of all the compromising that such relationships require. We get tired of giving up the things that mean so much to us.

"Turn off that noise you call music!"

"Why, so you can play more of the awful violin scratching?!"

Then, we go looking for someone whose values and interests and ideas are more like our own. We're just more comfortable together. If I truly love classical music, wouldn't I be happier sharing my life with someone who shared my love of classical music? And if my partner truly loved heavy metal, wouldn't she be happier with someone who also liked that sort of thing?

If you love Shabbat candles and Pesach seders,

building a sukkah and lighting the Hanukkah menorah, going to the synagogue on Rosh Hashanah to hear the shofar and to see old friends; if you love hamantaschen, latkes, fried matzah, apples and honey; if you think a lot about the Holocaust, about Israel, about Torah, wouldn't you be happier spending your life with someone who shared all this with you?

Here's another thought: There are 6 billion people in the world (that's 6 thousand million). Of that number, there are about 2 billion Christians, 1.3 billion Muslims, 900 million Hindus, and 360 million Buddhists. Guess how many Jews? From TV and other media, you might think there are a lot of us. But the truth is, there are only about 12 million Jews in the entire world. You do the math: 12 million Jews in a world of 6 billion people. We are a very small people.

The world population is growing, but the population of Jews is getting smaller. Before the Holocaust, there were 18 million Jews in the world. The Nazis murdered 6 million Jews, one-third of the world's Jews at the time. A large number of Americans who were born Jewish have nothing Jewish in their lives. They don't attend a synagogue, they don't give to Jewish charities, and they don't care to be Jewish in any way. By the time their kids grow up, they will have forgotten they are Jews.

Those of us who love being Jewish would like to see Judaism continue into the next generation. We believe being Jewish adds something very special to our lives. We hope our children and grandchildren will want to be Jewish so their lives will be special, too. We believe that Jews make important contributions to the world. Just count up all the great Jewish thinkers, scientists, artists, leaders, and performers. We hope there will be strong, proud Jews in the next generation to make their contributions to world civilization.

How can we best do this? How can we best assure that there will be people in the next generation who love being Jewish?

Of all the places that people learn to be Jewish, the most powerful place is at home. Synagogues, schools, summer camps, and trips to Israel are all important. But the most important place people learn to love being Jewish is in a Jewish home. And the best way to have a home that expresses a love for being Jewish is to share your home with a life partner who loves being Jewish.

This is not to say that it's impossible to learn to love being Jewish if one parent isn't Jewish. There are lots of Jews who have grown up with one Jewish parent and one parent of another faith. It can work, it's just harder. If one parent lights Shabbat candles, makes a seder, and belongs to a synagogue while the other parent attends church, puts up a Christmas tree, and prepares Easter dinner, it can be harder for a kid to grow up loving Judaism and living a Jewish life. It often puts him or her into the terrible position of choosing between parents and their faiths.

Because we want a new generation growing up loving Judaism and living a Jewish life, we hope that Jews will marry other Jews and build loving Jewish homes.

WHAT IF I FALL IN LOVE WITH A PERSON WHO ISN'T JEWISH BUT WANTS TO BE? CAN SOMEONE JOIN UP?

Since the time of Abraham and Sarah, the Jewish people have welcomed outsiders who wish to join us. When a person is interested in becoming Jewish, we ask that he or she take some serious time to learn the history, traditions, and teachings of Judaism. We ask that person to participate in the life of the synagogue and community. And we ask that person to give very serious thought to his or her beliefs and feelings. Many communities have a program set up to help people through this process.

At the end of the process, if the individual still wants to join the Jewish people, we present him or her to a *Beit Din*—a court of rabbis—for their approval. Then, there are rituals: circumcision and immersion into the *mikva* for men, immersion into the *mikva* for women. (Mikva is a ritual bath used by Jews for moments of transformation and renewal.)

Once a person has completed the learning process and these rituals, we give the person a Hebrew name and the designation *ben-* or *bat-Avraham v'Sarah*—children of Abraham and Sarah. These people are never called "converts." They are fully and completely Jewish and welcomed warmly into the Jewish community.

In the Bible, there is a story of a woman named Ruth. She marries a Jewish man who soon dies. When her husband's mother tells her to go home, go back to her people, she answers with great power and beauty:

> Don't tell me to leave you, to turn away and not follow you. Wherever you go, I will go. Where you live, I will live. Your people will be my people, and your God will be my God. Where you die, I will be buried. And nothing but death will separate me from you (Ruth 1:16–17).

Ruth remarried a member of her husband's family and had children. The Bible tells us that Ruth was the great-grandmother of King David, the greatest king of Israel, who is himself the ancestor of the Messiah. Recall that the Messiah represents the ultimate fixing of the world. We start the process of fixing the world when we welcome the outsider who wishes to become part of us.

18

Why Be Jewish?

The last week of our class came around. Most of the afternoon was spent rehearsing for a graduation ceremony. But in the last half-hour, we returned to the classroom for a class party. There were soda, chips, candy, and a huge cake baked by Jennifer and Molly.

"Listen Rabbi," Billy spoke up as everyone enjoyed the goodies. "You wouldn't mind if we talk today. It wouldn't seem right if we skipped it!"

I smiled and invited him to ask the last question of our class. Everyone quieted down as Billy formulated his thoughts. "I get the God thing," he began. "I even get prayer. And I really like that idea of being God's partner. But just so I don't mess up when I'm on the bimah at my Bar Mitzvah, tell me again. Why should I be Jewish?"

The biggest, most important job you have right now is writing the story of your life. You are its author, its illustrator, its publisher. You decide its plot, its themes, its lesson. You get to decide what's going to happen next. Some things in your life are beyond your control—how tall you'll be, for example. But much of your life's story is up to you to create. You have that power.

If you don't make the choice to shape your life carefully and with wisdom, there are forces all around that will do it for you. If you don't live life on purpose, you'll live by accident. The sad truth is that most people live by accident. They let life "happen" to them. And then one day, usually late in their years, they wake up to discover that they've missed all that life offered. They missed the chance to have dreams and plans and choices. They missed the chance to live a life that matters. That's a tragedy.

So, what's going to be the story of your life? What kind of life will you lead?

Here's my hope for you: Be a hero.

A hero need not be famous. A hero isn't just the firefighter who rushes into the burning building to save someone's cat. A hero is someone who has made his or her life into a symbol of something higher and greater. A hero is a person whose life matters.

"Don't just learn the Torah," taught the Hasidic master Menachem Mendel of Kotzk. "Be a Torah!" Make your whole life into a holy book, a sacred story. Make your whole life into a text that other people can read and learn from.

My friend Jonathan is a hero. All his work is about gaining knowledge to preserve and protect life. Mark is a hero. His life is a symbol and a champion of *Teshuva,* the power to change and choose good over evil and to teach others to choose life over death. Charles is a hero. His life stands for caring and healing.

Why be Jewish? Judaism teaches us how to live the life of a hero. As we've learned, being Jewish means accepting the most important responsibility there is.

Sharing God's dreams and working as God's partner to make the world whole is not easy. Mending the world is heroic work. It takes a lifetime of great courage and energy. It's a full-time job.

We learn Torah—the wisdom of the Jewish tradition—to hear God's voice and share God's dreams. Torah gives us the blueprint plan for building a world that's whole and peaceful.

We do mitzvot, the rituals and symbols of Jewish tradition, to get the skills and tools we'll need to repair the world: to bring peace where there's war, to bring healing where there's hurt, to bring hope where there's despair.

We pray to come close to God and get from God the strength and the courage to face a world that's such a mess.

We share life with a community. We remember the experiences of our ancestors, sharing their stories, their triumphs, and their tragedies, so that our work of mending the world isn't done alone.

The most important thing you can do with your life is to become God's partner.

Why be Jewish? To live a life of importance. To be a hero.

 *One More Thing*

I hope I've helped you wrestle with some important questions. Although these are the ones my students asked me, I'm sure that there are other questions we didn't get to. You'll find lots of other books that offer answers to those questions. You might also ask your rabbi or teacher for the kind of discussion we've shared in this book. Finally, I would appreciate hearing from you if you've found good answers to these questions, or if there are more questions you'd like to discuss. E-mail me: efeinstein@vbs.org. Thank you.

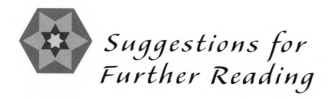 *Suggestions for Further Reading*

Artson, Bradley Shavit. *It's a Mitzvah: Step-by-Step to Jewish Living*. New York: Behrman House, 1995.

    This book invites us to live a joyful and meaningful Jewish life. It offers clear instructions and great explanations of Jewish rituals and practices.

Kushner, Harold. *To Life!: A Celebration of Jewish Being and Thinking*. New York: Warner Books, 1994.

    This book explains all of Judaism, its ideas, its way of living, and its dreams in a way that makes us want to learn more.

Kushner, Harold. *When Bad Things Happen to Good People*. New York: Avon Books, 2001.

    The most difficult of all questions is, why me? This book presents one of the best answers.

Kushner, Lawrence. *The Book of Miracles: A Young Person's Guide to Jewish Spiritual Awareness*. Woodstock, Vt.: Jewish Lights Publishing, 1997.

Combining the Talmud, midrash, and mystical and biblical stories, this book introduces us to the spiritual richness of the Jewish tradition.

Salkin, Jeffrey K. *For Kids—Putting God on Your Guest List*. Woodstock, Vt.: Jewish Lights Publishing, 1998.

Make your Bar or Bat Mitzvah more than just a thirteenth birthday party! This book will help.

Steinberg, Milton. *As a Driven Leaf*. New York: Behrman House, 1996.

This classic is an exciting historical novel exploring the beginning of Judaism in the days of the talmudic rabbis.

Wiesel, Elie. *Night*. New York: Bantam Books, 1982.

Winner of the Nobel Peace Prize, Elie Wiesel was taken to a Nazi concentration camp when he was just fifteen years old. This is his sad and powerful story.

About Jewish Lights

People of all faiths and backgrounds yearn for books that attract, engage, educate, and spiritually inspire.

Our principal goal is to stimulate thought and help all people learn about who the Jewish People are, where they come from, and what the future can be made to hold. While people of our diverse Jewish heritage are the primary audience, our books speak to people in the Christian world as well and will broaden their understanding of Judaism and the roots of their own faith.

We bring to you authors who are at the forefront of spiritual thought and experience. While each has something different to say, they all say it in a voice that you can hear.

Our books are designed to welcome you and then to engage, stimulate, and inspire. We judge our success not only by whether or not our books are beautiful and commercially successful, but by whether or not they make a difference in your life.

For your information and convenience, at the back of this book we have provided a list of other Jewish Lights books you might find interesting and useful. They cover all the categories of your life:

Bar/Bat Mitzvah
Bible Study / Midrash
Children's Books
Congregation Resources
Current Events / History
Ecology
Fiction: Mystery, Science Fiction
Grief / Healing
Holidays / Holy Days
Inspiration
Kabbalah / Mysticism / Enneagram

Life Cycle
Meditation
Parenting
Prayer
Ritual / Sacred Practice
Spirituality
Theology / Philosophy
Travel
Twelve Steps
Women's Interest

Stuart M. Matlins, Publisher

Or phone, fax, mail or e-mail to: **JEWISH LIGHTS Publishing**
Sunset Farm Offices, Route 4 • P.O. Box 237 • Woodstock, Vermont 05091
Tel: (802) 457-4000 • Fax: (802) 457-4004 • www.jewishlights.com
Credit card orders: (800) 962-4544 (8:30AM–5:30PM ET Monday–Friday)
Generous discounts on quantity orders. SATISFACTION GUARANTEED. Prices subject to change.

Theology/Philosophy

Aspects of Rabbinic Theology
By Solomon Schechter. New Introduction by Dr. Neil Gillman.
6 x 9, 448 pp, Quality PB, ISBN 1-879045-24-9 **$19.95**

Broken Tablets: Restoring the Ten Commandments and Ourselves
Edited by Rachel S. Mikva. Introduction by Lawrence Kushner. Afterword by Arnold Jacob Wolf.
6 x 9, 192 pp, Quality PB, ISBN 1-58023-158-6 **$16.95**; Hardcover, ISBN 1-58023-066-0 **$21.95**

Creating an Ethical Jewish Life
A Practical Introduction to Classic Teachings on How to Be a Jew
By Dr. Byron L. Sherwin and Seymour J. Cohen
6 x 9, 336 pp, Quality PB, ISBN 1-58023-114-4 **$19.95**

The Death of Death: Resurrection and Immortality in Jewish Thought
By Dr. Neil Gillman 6 x 9, 336 pp, Quality PB, ISBN 1-58023-081-4 **$18.95**

Evolving Halakhah: A Progressive Approach to Traditional Jewish Law
By Rabbi Dr. Moshe Zemer
6 x 9, 480 pp, Quality PB, ISBN 1-58023-127-6 **$29.95**; Hardcover, ISBN 1-58023-002-4 **$40.00**

Hasidic Tales: Annotated & Explained
By Rabbi Rami Shapiro. Foreword by Andrew Harvey, SkyLight Illuminations series editor.
5½ x 8½, 240 pp, Quality PB, ISBN 1-893361-86-1 **$16.95** (A SkyLight Paths Book)

A Heart of Many Rooms: Celebrating the Many Voices within Judaism
By Dr. David Hartman 6 x 9, 352 pp, Quality PB, ISBN 1-58023-156-X **$19.95**

The Hebrew Prophets: Selections Annotated & Explained
Translation & Annotation by Rabbi Rami Shapiro. Foreword by Zalman M. Schachter-Shalomi
5½ x 8½, 224 pp, Quality PB, ISBN 1-59473-037-7 **$16.99** (A SkyLight Paths book)

Keeping Faith with the Psalms: Deepen Your Relationship with God Using the
Book of Psalms By Daniel F. Polish 6 x 9, 272 pp, Hardcover, ISBN 1-58023-179-9 **$24.95**

The Last Trial
On the Legends and Lore of the Command to Abraham to Offer Isaac as a Sacrifice
By Shalom Spiegel. New Introduction by Judah Goldin.
6 x 9, 208 pp, Quality PB, ISBN 1-879045-29-X **$18.95**

A Living Covenant: The Innovative Spirit in Traditional Judaism
By Dr. David Hartman 6 x 9, 368 pp, Quality PB, ISBN 1-58023-011-3 **$18.95**

Love and Terror in the God Encounter
The Theological Legacy of Rabbi Joseph B. Soloveitchik
By Dr. David Hartman
6 x 9, 240 pp, Quality PB, ISBN 1-58023-176-4 **$19.95**; Hardcover, ISBN 1-58023-112-8 **$25.00**

Seeking the Path to Life
Theological Meditations on God and the Nature of People, Love, Life and Death
By Rabbi Ira F. Stone 6 x 9, 160 pp, Quality PB, ISBN 1-879045-47-8 **$14.95**

The Spirit of Renewal: Finding Faith after the Holocaust
By Rabbi Edward Feld 6 x 9, 224 pp, Quality PB, ISBN 1-879045-40-0 **$16.95**

Tormented Master: The Life and Spiritual Quest of Rabbi Nahman of Bratslav
By Dr. Arthur Green 6 x 9, 416 pp, Quality PB, ISBN 1-879045-11-7 **$19.99**

Your Word Is Fire: The Hasidic Masters on Contemplative Prayer
Edited and translated by Dr. Arthur Green and Barry W. Holtz
6 x 9, 160 pp, Quality PB, ISBN 1-879045-25-7 **$15.95**

I Am Jewish
Personal Reflections Inspired by the Last Words of Daniel Pearl
Almost 150 Jews—both famous and not—from all walks of life, from all around
the world, write about Identity, Heritage, Covenant / Chosenness and Faith,
Humanity and Ethnicity, and *Tikkun Olam* and Justice.
Edited by Judea and Ruth Pearl
6 x 9, 304 pp, Deluxe PB w/flaps, ISBN 1-58023-259-0 **$18.99**; Hardcover, ISBN 1-58023-183-7 **$24.99**
Download a free copy of the *I Am Jewish Teacher's Guide* at our website:
www.jewishlights.com

Inspiration

God in All Moments
Mystical & Practical Spiritual Wisdom from Hasidic Masters
Edited and translated by Or N. Rose with Ebn D. Leader
Hasidic teachings on how to be mindful in religious practice and cultivating everyday ethical behavior—*hanhagot*. 5½ x 8½, 192 pp, Quality PB, ISBN 1-58023-186-1 **$16.95**

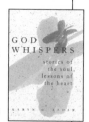

Our Dance with God: Finding Prayer, Perspective and Meaning in the
Stories of Our Lives *By Karyn D. Kedar*
Inspiring spiritual insight to guide you on your life journeys and teach you to live and thrive in two conflicting worlds: the rational/material and the spiritual.
6 x 9, 176 pp, Quality PB, ISBN 1-58023-202-7 **$16.99**

Also Available: **The Dance of the Dolphin** (Hardcover edition of *Our Dance with God*)
6 x 9, 176 pp, Hardcover, ISBN 1-58023-154-3 **$19.95**

The Empty Chair: Finding Hope and Joy—Timeless Wisdom from a Hasidic Master,
Rebbe Nachman of Breslov *Adapted by Moshe Mykoff and the Breslov Research Institute*
4 x 6, 128 pp, 2-color text, Deluxe PB w/flaps, ISBN 1-879045-67-2 **$9.95**

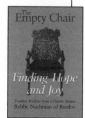

The Gentle Weapon: Prayers for Everyday and Not-So-Everyday Moments—
Timeless Wisdom from the Teachings of the Hasidic Master, Rebbe Nachman of Breslov
Adapted by Moshe Mykoff and S. C. Mizrahi, together with the Breslov Research Institute
4 x 6, 144 pp, 2-color text, Deluxe PB w/flaps, ISBN 1-58023-022-9 **$9.95**

God Whispers: Stories of the Soul, Lessons of the Heart *By Karyn D. Kedar*
6 x 9, 176 pp, Quality PB, ISBN 1-58023-088-1 **$15.95**

An Orphan in History: One Man's Triumphant Search for His Jewish Roots
By Paul Cowan. Afterword by Rachel Cowan. 6 x 9, 288 pp, Quality PB, ISBN 1-58023-135-7 **$16.95**

Restful Reflections: Nighttime Inspiration to Calm the Soul, Based on Jewish Wisdom
By Rabbi Kerry M. Olitzky & Rabbi Lori Forman 4½ x 6½, 448 pp, Quality PB, ISBN 1-58023-091-1 **$15.95**

Sacred Intentions: Daily Inspiration to Strengthen the Spirit, Based on Jewish Wisdom
By Rabbi Kerry M. Olitzky and Rabbi Lori Forman 4½ x 6½, 448 pp, Quality PB, ISBN 1-58023-061-X **$15.95**

Kabbalah/Mysticism/Enneagram

Seek My Face: A Jewish Mystical Theology
By Dr. Arthur Green
This classic work of contemporary Jewish theology, revised and updated, is a profound, deeply personal statement of the lasting truths of Jewish mysticism and the basic faith claims of Judaism. A tool for anyone seeking the elusive presence of God in the world. 6 x 9, 304 pp, Quality PB, ISBN 1-58023-130-6 **$19.95**

Zohar: Annotated & Explained
Translation and annotation by Dr. Daniel C. Matt. Foreword by Andrew Harvey
Offers insightful yet unobtrusive commentary to the masterpiece of Jewish mysticism. Explains references and mystical symbols, shares wisdom of spiritual masters, and clarifies the *Zohar*'s bold claim: We have always been taught that we need God, but in order to manifest in the world, God needs us.
5½ x 8½, 160 pp, Quality PB, ISBN 1-893361-51-9 **$15.99** *(A SkyLight Paths book)*

Cast in God's Image: Discover Your Personality Type Using the Enneagram and Kabbalah
By Rabbi Howard A. Addison
7 x 9, 176 pp, Quality PB, Layflat binding, 20+ journaling exercises, ISBN 1-58023-124-1 **$16.95**

Ehyeh: A Kabbalah for Tomorrow *By Dr. Arthur Green*
6 x 9, 224 pp, Quality PB, ISBN 1-58023-213-2 **$16.99**; Hardcover, ISBN 1-58023-125-X **$21.95**

The Enneagram and Kabbalah: Reading Your Soul *By Rabbi Howard A. Addison*
6 x 9, 176 pp, Quality PB, ISBN 1-58023-001-6 **$15.95**

Finding Joy: A Practical Spiritual Guide to Happiness *By Dannel I. Schwartz with Mark Hass*
6 x 9, 192 pp, Quality PB, ISBN 1-58023-009-1 **$14.95**

The Gift of Kabbalah: Discovering the Secrets of Heaven, Renewing Your Life on Earth
By Tamar Frankiel, Ph.D.
6 x 9, 256 pp, Quality PB, ISBN 1-58023-141-1 **$16.95**; Hardcover, ISBN 1-58023-108-X **$21.95**

The Way Into Jewish Mystical Tradition *By Lawrence Kushner*
6 x 9, 224 pp, Quality PB, ISBN 1-58023-200-0 **$18.99**; Hardcover, ISBN 1-58023-029-6 **$21.95**

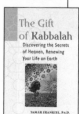

Spirituality

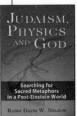

Does the Soul Survive?: A Jewish Journey to Belief in Afterlife, Past Lives & Living with Purpose *By Rabbi Elie Kaplan Spitz. Foreword by Brian L Weiss, M.D.*
Spitz relates his own experiences and those shared with him by people he has worked with as a rabbi, and shows us that belief in afterlife and past lives, so often approached with reluctance, is in fact true to Jewish tradition.
6 x 9, 288 pp, Quality PB, ISBN 1-58023-165-9 **$16.95**; Hardcover, ISBN 1-58023-094-6 **$21.95**

First Steps to a New Jewish Spirit: Reb Zalman's Guide to Recapturing the Intimacy & Ecstasy in Your Relationship with God
By Rabbi Zalman M. Schachter-Shalomi with Donald Gropman
An extraordinary spiritual handbook that restores psychic and physical vigor by introducing us to new models and alternative ways of practicing Judaism. Offers meditation and contemplation exercises for enriching the most important aspects of everyday life. 6 x 9, 144 pp, Quality PB, ISBN 1-58023-182-9 **$16.95**

God in Our Relationships: Spirituality between People from the Teachings of Martin Buber *By Rabbi Dennis S. Ross*
On the eightieth anniversary of Buber's classic work, we can discover new answers to critical issues in our lives. Inspiring examples from Ross's own life—as congregational rabbi, father, hospital chaplain, social worker, and husband—illustrate Buber's difficult-to-understand ideas about how we encounter God and each other. 5½ x 8½, 160 pp, Quality PB, ISBN 1-58023-147-0 **$16.95**

Judaism, Physics and God: Searching for Sacred Metaphors in a Post-Einstein World *By Rabbi David W. Nelson*
In clear, non-technical terms, this provocative fusion of religion and science examines the great theories of modern physics to find new ways for contemporary people to express their spiritual beliefs and thoughts.
6 x 9, 352 pp, Hardcover, ISBN 1-58023-252-3 **$24.99**

The Jewish Lights Spirituality Handbook: A Guide to Understanding, Exploring & Living a Spiritual Life *Edited by Stuart M. Matlins*
What exactly is "Jewish" about spirituality? How do I make it a part of my life? Fifty of today's foremost spiritual leaders share their ideas and experience with us.
6 x 9, 456 pp, Quality PB, ISBN 1-58023-093-8 **$19.95**; Hardcover, ISBN 1-58023-100-4 **$24.95**

Bringing the Psalms to Life: How to Understand and Use the Book of Psalms
By Dr. Daniel F. Polish
6 x 9, 208 pp, Quality PB, ISBN 1-58023-157-8 **$16.95**; Hardcover, ISBN 1-58023-077-6 **$21.95**

God & the Big Bang: Discovering Harmony between Science & Spirituality
By Dr. Daniel C. Matt 6 x 9, 216 pp, Quality PB, ISBN 1-879045-89-3 **$16.95**

Godwrestling—Round 2: Ancient Wisdom, Future Paths
By Rabbi Arthur Waskow 6 x 9, 352 pp, Quality PB, ISBN 1-879045-72-9 **$18.95**

One God Clapping: The Spiritual Path of a Zen Rabbi *By Rabbi Alan Lew with Sherril Jaffe*
5½ x 8½, 336 pp, Quality PB, ISBN 1-58023-115-2 **$16.95**

The Path of Blessing: Experiencing the Energy and Abundance of the Divine
By Rabbi Marcia Prager 5½ x 8½, 240 pp., Quality PB, ISBN 1-58023-148-9 **$16.95**

Six Jewish Spiritual Paths: A Rationalist Looks at Spirituality *By Rabbi Rifat Sonsino*
6 x 9, 208 pp, Quality PB, ISBN 1-58023-167-5 **$16.95**; Hardcover, ISBN 1-58023-095-4 **$21.95**

Soul Judaism: Dancing with God into a New Era
By Rabbi Wayne Dosick 5½ x 8½, 304 pp, Quality PB, ISBN 1-58023-053-9 **$16.95**

Stepping Stones to Jewish Spiritual Living: Walking the Path Morning, Noon, and Night *By Rabbi James L. Mirel and Karen Bonnell Werth*
6 x 9, 240 pp, Quality PB, ISBN 1-58023-074-1 **$16.95**; Hardcover, ISBN 1-58023-003-2 **$21.95**

There Is No Messiah... and You're It: The Stunning Transformation of Judaism's Most Provocative Idea *By Rabbi Robert N. Levine, D.D.*
6 x 9, 192 pp, Quality PB, ISBN 1-58023-255-8 **$16.99**; Hardcover, ISBN 1-58023-173-X **$21.95**

These Are the Words: A Vocabulary of Jewish Spiritual Life *By Dr. Arthur Green*
6 x 9, 304 pp, Quality PB, ISBN 1-58023-107-1 **$18.95**

Spirituality/Lawrence Kushner

Filling Words with Light: Hasidic and Mystical Reflections on Jewish Prayer
By Lawrence Kushner and Nehemia Polen
Reflects on the joy, gratitude, mystery, and awe embedded in traditional prayers and blessings, and shows how you can imbue these familiar sacred words with your own sense of holiness. 5½ x 8½, 176 pp, Hardcover, ISBN 1-58023-216-7 **$21.99**

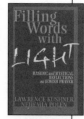

The Book of Letters: A Mystical Hebrew Alphabet
Popular Hardcover Edition, 6 x 9, 80 pp, 2-color text, ISBN 1-879045-00-1 **$24.95**
Collector's Limited Edition, 9 x 12, 80 pp, gold foil embossed pages, w/limited edition silkscreened print, ISBN 1-879045-04-4 **$349.00**

The Book of Miracles: A Young Person's Guide to Jewish Spiritual Awareness
6 x 9, 96 pp, 2-color illus., Hardcover, ISBN 1-879045-78-8 **$16.95** *For ages 9–13*

The Book of Words: Talking Spiritual Life, Living Spiritual Talk
6 x 9, 160 pp, Quality PB, ISBN 1-58023-020-2 **$16.95**

Eyes Remade for Wonder: A Lawrence Kushner Reader *Introduction by Thomas Moore*
6 x 9, 240 pp, Quality PB, ISBN 1-58023-042-3 **$18.95;** Hardcover, ISBN 1-58023-014-8 **$23.95**

God Was in This Place & I, i Did Not Know
Finding Self, Spirituality and Ultimate Meaning 6 x 9, 192 pp, Quality PB, ISBN 1-879045-33-8 **$16.95**

Honey from the Rock: An Introduction to Jewish Mysticism
6 x 9, 176 pp, Quality PB, ISBN 1-58023-073-3 **$16.95**

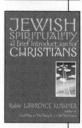

Invisible Lines of Connection: Sacred Stories of the Ordinary
5½ x 8½, 160 pp, Quality PB, ISBN 1-879045-98-2 **$15.95**

Jewish Spirituality—A Brief Introduction for Christians
5½ x 8½, 112 pp, Quality PB Original, ISBN 1-58023-150-0 **$12.95**

The River of Light: Jewish Mystical Awareness 6 x 9, 192 pp, Quality PB, ISBN 1-58023-096-2 **$16.95**

The Way Into Jewish Mystical Tradition
6 x 9, 224 pp, Quality PB, ISBN 1-58023-200-0 **$18.99;** Hardcover, ISBN 1-58023-029-6 **$21.95**

Spirituality/Prayer

Pray Tell: A Hadassah Guide to Jewish Prayer
By Rabbi Jules Harlow, with contributions from Tamara Cohen, Rochelle Furstenberg, Rabbi Daniel Gordis, Leora Tanenbaum, and many others
A guide to traditional Jewish prayer enriched with insight and wisdom from a broad variety of viewpoints—from Orthodox, Conservative, Reform, and Reconstructionist Judaism to New Age and feminist.
8½ x 11, 400 pp, Quality PB, ISBN 1-58023-163-2 **$29.95**

My People's Prayer Book Series
Traditional Prayers, Modern Commentaries *Edited by Rabbi Lawrence A. Hoffman*
Provides diverse and exciting commentary to the traditional liturgy, helping modern men and women find new wisdom in Jewish prayer, and bring liturgy into their lives. Each book includes Hebrew text, modern translation, and commentaries from all perspectives of the Jewish world.

Vol. 1—The *Sh'ma* and Its Blessings
   7 x 10, 168 pp, Hardcover, ISBN 1-879045-79-6 **$23.95**
Vol. 2—The *Amidah*
   7 x 10, 240 pp, Hardcover, ISBN 1-879045-80-X **$24.95**
Vol. 3—*P'sukei D'zimrah* (Morning Psalms)
   7 x 10, 240 pp, Hardcover, ISBN 1-879045-81-8 **$24.95**
Vol. 4—*Seder K'riat Hatorah* (The Torah Service)
   7 x 10, 264 pp, Hardcover, ISBN 1-879045-82-6 **$23.95**
Vol. 5—*Birkhot Hashachar* (Morning Blessings)
   7 x 10, 240 pp, Hardcover, ISBN 1-879045-83-4 **$24.95**
Vol. 6—*Tachanun* and Concluding Prayers
   7 x 10, 240 pp, Hardcover, ISBN 1-879045-84-2 **$24.95**
Vol. 7—Shabbat at Home
   7 x 10, 240 pp, Hardcover, ISBN 1-879045-85-0 **$24.95**
Vol. 8—*Kabbalat Shabbat* (Welcoming Shabbat in the Synagogue)
   7 x 10, 240 pp, Hardcover, ISBN 1-58023-121-7 **$24.99**

Spirituality/The Way Into... Series

The Way Into... Series offers an accessible and highly usable "guided tour" of the Jewish faith, people, history and beliefs—in total, an introduction to Judaism that will enable you to understand and interact with the sacred texts of the Jewish tradition. Each volume is written by a leading contemporary scholar and teacher, and explores one key aspect of Judaism. *The Way Into...* enables all readers to achieve a real sense of Jewish cultural literacy through guided study.

The Way Into Encountering God in Judaism *By Neil Gillman*
6 x 9, 240 pp, Quality PB, ISBN 1-58023-199-3 **$18.99**; Hardcover, ISBN 1-58023-025-3 **$21.95**

Also Available: **The Jewish Approach to God: A Brief Introduction for Christians**
By Neil Gillman 5½ x 8½, 192 pp, Quality PB, ISBN 1-58023-190-X **$16.95**

The Way Into Jewish Mystical Tradition *By Lawrence Kushner*
6 x 9, 224 pp, Quality PB, ISBN 1-58023-200-0 **$18.99**; Hardcover, ISBN 1-58023-029-6 **$21.95**

The Way Into Jewish Prayer *By Lawrence A. Hoffman*
6 x 9, 224 pp, Quality PB, ISBN 1-58023-201-9 **$18.99**; Hardcover, ISBN 1-58023-027-X **$21.95**

The Way Into Torah *By Norman J. Cohen*
6 x 9, 176 pp, Quality PB, ISBN 1-58023-198-5 **$16.99**; Hardcover, ISBN 1-58023-028-8 **$21.95**

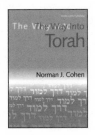

Spirituality in the Workplace

Being God's Partner
How to Find the Hidden Link Between Spirituality and Your Work
By Rabbi Jeffrey K. Salkin. Introduction by Norman Lear.
6 x 9, 192 pp, Quality PB, ISBN 1-879045-65-6 **$17.95**

The Business Bible: 10 New Commandments for Bringing Spirituality & Ethical Values into the Workplace *By Rabbi Wayne Dosick*
5½ x 8½, 208 pp, Quality PB, ISBN 1-58023-101-2 **$14.95**

Spirituality and Wellness

Aleph-Bet Yoga
Embodying the Hebrew Letters for Physical and Spiritual Well-Being
By Steven A. Rapp. Foreword by Tamar Frankiel, Ph.D., and Judy Greenfeld. Preface by Hart Lazer
7 x 10, 128 pp, b/w photos, Quality PB, Layflat binding, ISBN 1-58023-162-4 **$16.95**

Entering the Temple of Dreams
Jewish Prayers, Movements, and Meditations for the End of the Day
By Tamar Frankiel, Ph.D., and Judy Greenfeld
7 x 10, 192 pp, illus., Quality PB, ISBN 1-58023-079-2 **$16.95**

Jewish Paths toward Healing and Wholeness: A Personal Guide to Dealing with Suffering *By Rabbi Kerry M. Olitzky. Foreword by Debbie Friedman.*
6 x 9, 192 pp, Quality PB, ISBN 1-58023-068-7 **$15.95**

Minding the Temple of the Soul
Balancing Body, Mind, and Spirit through Traditional Jewish Prayer, Movement, and Meditation *By Tamar Frankiel, Ph.D., and Judy Greenfeld*
7 x 10, 184 pp, illus., Quality PB, ISBN 1-879045-64-8 **$16.95**
Audiotape of the Blessings and Meditations: 60 min. **$9.95**
Videotape of the Movements and Meditations: 46 min. **$20.00**

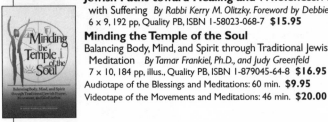

Current Events/History

The Story of the Jews: A 4,000-Year Adventure—A Graphic History Book
Written & illustrated by Stan Mack
Witty, illustrated narrative of all the major happenings from biblical times to the twenty-first century.   6 x 9, 288 pp, illus., Quality PB, ISBN 1-58023-155-1 **$16.95**

Hannah Senesh: Her Life and Diary, the First Complete Edition
By Hannah Senesh; Foreword by Marge Piercy; Preface by Eitan Senesh
6 x 9, 352 pp, Hardcover, ISBN 1-58023-212-4 **$24.99**

The Jewish Prophet: Visionary Words from Moses and Miriam to Henrietta Szold and A. J. Heschel   *By Rabbi Michael J. Shire*
6½ x 8½, 128 pp, 123 full-color illus., Hardcover, ISBN 1-58023-168-3 **Special gift price $14.95**

Shared Dreams: Martin Luther King, Jr. & the Jewish Community
By Rabbi Marc Schneier. Preface by Martin Luther King III.
6 x 9, 240 pp, Hardcover, ISBN 1-58023-062-8 **$24.95**

"Who Is a Jew?": Conversations, Not Conclusions   *By Meryl Hyman*
6 x 9, 272 pp, Quality PB, ISBN 1-58023-052-0 **$16.95**

Ecology

Ecology & the Jewish Spirit: Where Nature & the Sacred Meet
Edited by Ellen Bernstein   6 x 9, 288 pp, Quality PB, ISBN 1-58023-082-2 **$16.95**

Torah of the Earth: Exploring 4,000 Years of Ecology in Jewish Thought
Vol. 1: Biblical Israel: One Land, One People; Rabbinic Judaism: One People, Many Lands
Vol. 2: Zionism: One Land, Two Peoples; Eco-Judaism: One Earth, Many Peoples
Edited by Rabbi Arthur Waskow
Vol. 1: 6 x 9, 272 pp, Quality PB, ISBN 1-58023-086-5 **$19.95**
Vol. 2: 6 x 9, 336 pp, Quality PB, ISBN 1-58023-087-3 **$19.95**

Grief/Healing

Against the Dying of the Light: A Parent's Story of Love, Loss and Hope
By Leonard Fein
Unusual exploration of heartbreak and healing. Chronicles the sudden death of author's 30-year-old daughter and shares the wisdom that emerges in the face of loss and grief.
5½ x 8½, 176 pp, Quality PB, ISBN 1-58023-197-7 **$15.99;** Hardcover, ISBN 1-58023-110-1 **$19.95**

Grief in Our Seasons: A Mourner's Kaddish Companion   *By Rabbi Kerry M. Olitzky*
4½ x 6½, 448 pp, Quality PB, ISBN 1-879045-55-9 **$15.95**

Healing of Soul, Healing of Body: Spiritual Leaders Unfold the Strength & Solace in Psalms   *Edited by Rabbi Simkha Y. Weintraub, C.S.W.*
6 x 9, 128 pp, 2-color illus. text, Quality PB, ISBN 1-879045-31-1 **$14.95**

Jewish Paths toward Healing and Wholeness: A Personal Guide to Dealing with Suffering   *By Rabbi Kerry M. Olitzky. Foreword by Debbie Friedman.*
6 x 9, 192 pp, Quality PB, ISBN 1-58023-068-7 **$15.95**

Mourning & Mitzvah, 2nd Edition: A Guided Journal for Walking the Mourner's Path through Grief to Healing   *By Anne Brener, L.C.S.W.*
7½ x 9, 304 pp, Quality PB, ISBN 1-58023-113-6 **$19.95**

The Perfect Stranger's Guide to Funerals and Grieving Practices
A Guide to Etiquette in Other People's Religious Ceremonies   *Edited by Stuart M. Matlins*
6 x 9, 240 pp, Quality PB, ISBN 1-893361-20-9 **$16.95**   *(A SkyLight Paths book)*

Tears of Sorrow, Seeds of Hope: A Jewish Spiritual Companion for Infertility and Pregnancy Loss   *By Rabbi Nina Beth Cardin*
6 x 9, 192 pp, Hardcover, ISBN 1-58023-017-2 **$19.95**

A Time to Mourn, A Time to Comfort, 2nd Edition: A Guide to Jewish Bereavement and Comfort   *By Dr. Ron Wolfson*
7 x 9, 336 pp, Quality PB, ISBN 1-58023-253-1 **$19.99**

When a Grandparent Dies: A Kid's Own Remembering Workbook for Dealing with Shiva and the Year Beyond   *By Nechama Liss-Levinson, Ph.D.*
8 x 10, 48 pp, 2-color text, Hardcover, ISBN 1-879045-44-3 **$15.95**   *For ages 7–13*

Children's Books
by Sandy Eisenberg Sasso

Adam & Eve's First Sunset: God's New Day
Engaging new story explores fear and hope, faith and gratitude in ways that will delight kids and adults—inspiring us to bless each of God's days and nights.
9 x 12, 32 pp, Full-color illus., Hardcover, ISBN 1-58023-177-2 **$17.95** *For ages 4 & up*

But God Remembered
Stories of Women from Creation to the Promised Land
Four different stories of women—Lillith, Serach, Bityah, and the Daughters of Z—teach us important values through their faith and actions.
9 x 12, 32 pp, Full-color illus., Hardcover, ISBN 1-879045-43-5 **$16.95** *For ages 8 & up*

Cain & Abel: Finding the Fruits of Peace
Shows children that we have the power to deal with anger in positive ways. Provides questions for kids and adults to explore together.
9 x 12, 32 pp, Full-color illus., Hardcover, ISBN 1-58023-123-3 **$16.95** *For ages 5 & up*

God in Between
If you wanted to find God, where would you look? This magical, mythical tale teaches that God can be found where we are: within all of us and the relationships between us.
9 x 12, 32 pp, Full-color illus., Hardcover, ISBN 1-879045-86-9 **$16.95** *For ages 4 & up*

God's Paintbrush: Special 10th Anniversary Edition
Wonderfully interactive, invites children of all faiths and backgrounds to encounter God through moments in their own lives. Provides questions adult and child can explore together.
11 x 8½, 32 pp, Full-color illus., Hardcover, ISBN 1-58023-195-0 **$17.95** *For ages 4 & up*

Also Available: **God's Paintbrush Teacher's Guide**
8½ x 11, 32 pp, PB, ISBN 1-879045-57-5 **$8.95**

God's Paintbrush Celebration Kit
A Spiritual Activity Kit for Teachers and Students of All Faiths, All Backgrounds
Additional activity sheets available:
8-Student Activity Sheet Pack (40 sheets/5 sessions), ISBN 1-58023-058-X **$19.95**
Single-Student Activity Sheet Pack (5 sessions), ISBN 1-58023-059-8 **$3.95**

In God's Name
Like an ancient myth in its poetic text and vibrant illustrations, this award-winning modern fable about the search for God's name celebrates the diversity and, at the same time, the unity of all people.
9 x 12, 32 pp, Full-color illus., Hardcover, ISBN 1-879045-26-5 **$16.99** *For ages 4 & up*

Also Available as a Board Book: **What Is God's Name?**
5 x 5, 24 pp, Board, Full-color illus., ISBN 1-893361-10-1 **$7.99** *For ages 0–4 (A SkyLight Paths book)*

Also Available: **In God's Name video and study guide**
Computer animation, original music, and children's voices. 18 min. **$29.99**

Also Available in Spanish: **El nombre de Dios**
9 x 12, 32 pp, Full-color illus., Hardcover, ISBN 1-893361-63-2 **$16.95** *(A SkyLight Paths book)*

Noah's Wife: The Story of Naamah
When God tells Noah to bring the animals of the world onto the ark, God also calls on Naamah, Noah's wife, to save each plant on Earth. Based on an ancient text.
9 x 12, 32 pp, Full-color illus., Hardcover, ISBN 1-58023-134-9 **$16.95** *For ages 4 & up*

Also Available as a Board Book: **Naamah, Noah's Wife**
5 x 5, 24 pp, Full-color illus., Board, ISBN 1-893361-56-X **$7.95** *For ages 0–4 (A SkyLight Paths book)*

For Heaven's Sake: Finding God in Unexpected Places
9 x 12, 32 pp, Full-color illus., Hardcover, ISBN 1-58023-054-7 **$16.95** *For ages 4 & up*

God Said Amen: Finding the Answers to Our Prayers
9 x 12, 32 pp, Full-color illus., Hardcover, ISBN 1-58023-080-6 **$16.95** *For ages 4 & up*

Children's Books

What You Will See Inside a Synagogue
By Rabbi Lawrence A. Hoffman and Dr. Ron Wolfson; Full-color photos by Bill Aron
A colorful, fun-to-read introduction that explains the ways and whys of
Jewish worship and religious life. Full-page photos; concise but informative
descriptions of the objects used, the clergy and laypeople who have specific
roles, and much more. For ages 6 & up.
8½ x 10½, 32 pp, Full-color photos, Hardcover, ISBN 1-59473-012-1 **$17.99** *(A SkyLight Paths book)*

Because Nothing Looks Like God
By Lawrence and Karen Kushner
What is God like? Introduces children to the possibilities of spiritual life. Real-life
examples of happiness and sadness invite us to explore, together with our children, the questions we all have about God.
11 x 8½, 32 pp, Full-color illus., Hardcover, ISBN 1-58023-092-X **$16.95** *For ages 4 & up*

Also Available: **Because Nothing Looks Like God Teacher's Guide**
8½ x 11, 22 pp, PB, ISBN 1-58023-140-3 **$6.95** *For ages 5–8*
        Board Book Companions to *Because Nothing Looks Like God*
5 x 5, 24 pp, Full-color illus., SkyLight Paths Board Books, **$7.95** each *For ages 0–4*
What Does God Look Like? ISBN 1-893361-23-3
How Does God Make Things Happen? ISBN 1-893361-24-1
Where Is God? ISBN 1-893361-17-9

The 11th Commandment: Wisdom from Our Children
by The Children of America
"If there were an Eleventh Commandment, what would it be?" Children of many
religious denominations across America answer in their own drawings and words.
8 x 10, 48 pp, Full-color illus., Hardcover, ISBN 1-879045-46-X **$16.95** *For all ages*

Jerusalem of Gold: Jewish Stories of the Enchanted City
Retold by Howard Schwartz. Full-color illus. by Neil Waldman.
A beautiful and engaging collection of historical and legendary stories for children. Based on Talmud, midrash, Jewish folklore, and mystical and Hasidic sources.
8 x 10, 64 pp, Full-color illus., Hardcover, ISBN 1-58023-149-7 **$18.95** *For ages 7 & up*

The Book of Miracles: A Young Person's Guide to Jewish Spiritual Awareness
By Lawrence Kushner. All-new illustrations by the author.
6 x 9, 96 pp, 2-color illus., Hardcover, ISBN 1-879045-78-8 **$16.95** *For ages 9–13*

In Our Image: God's First Creatures
By Nancy Sohn Swartz
9 x 12, 32 pp, Full-color illus., Hardcover, ISBN 1-879045-99-0 **$16.95** *For ages 4 & up*

Also Available as a Board Book: **How Did the Animals Help God?**
5 x 5, 24 pp, Board, Full-color illus., ISBN 1-59473-044-X **$7.99** *For ages 0–4 (A SkyLight Paths book)*

From SKYLIGHT PATHS PUBLISHING

Becoming Me: A Story of Creation
By Martin Boroson. Full-color illus. by Christopher Gilvan-Cartwright.
Told in the personal "voice" of the Creator, a story about creation and relationship that is about each one of us.
8 x 10, 32 pp, Full-color illus., Hardcover, ISBN 1-893361-11-X **$16.95** *For ages 4 & up*

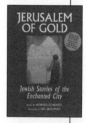

Ten Amazing People: And How They Changed the World
By Maura D. Shaw. Foreword by Dr. Robert Coles. Full-color illus. by Stephen Marchesi.
Black Elk • Dorothy Day • Malcolm X • Mahatma Gandhi • Martin Luther King,
Jr. • Mother Teresa • Janusz Korczak • Desmond Tutu • Thich Nhat Hanh •
Albert Schweitzer.
8½ x 11, 48 pp, Full-color illus., Hardcover, ISBN 1-893361-47-0 **$17.95** *For ages 7 & up*

Where Does God Live? *By August Gold and Matthew J. Perlman*
Helps young readers develop a personal understanding of God.
10 x 8½, 32 pp, Full-color photo illus., Quality PB, ISBN 1-893361-39-X **$8.99** *For ages 3–6*

Meditation

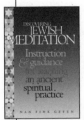

The Handbook of Jewish Meditation Practices
A Guide for Enriching the Sabbath and Other Days of Your Life
By Rabbi David A. Cooper
Easy-to-learn meditation techniques. 6 x 9, 208 pp, Quality PB, ISBN 1-58023-102-0 **$16.95**

Discovering Jewish Meditation: Instruction & Guidance for Learning an Ancient
Spiritual Practice By Nan Fink Gefen, Ph.D. 6 x 9, 208 pp, Quality PB, ISBN 1-58023-067-9 **$16.95**

A Heart of Stillness: A Complete Guide to Learning the Art of Meditation
By Rabbi David A. Cooper 5½ x 8½, 272 pp, Quality PB, ISBN 1-893361-03-9 **$16.95**
(A SkyLight Paths book)

Meditation from the Heart of Judaism: Today's Teachers Share Their
Practices, Techniques, and Faith Edited by Avram Davis
6 x 9, 256 pp, Quality PB, ISBN 1-58023-049-0 **$16.95**

Silence, Simplicity & Solitude: A Complete Guide to Spiritual Retreat at Home
By Rabbi David A. Cooper 5½ x 8½, 336 pp, Quality PB, ISBN 1-893361-04-7 **$16.95**
(A SkyLight Paths book)

The Way of Flame: A Guide to the Forgotten Mystical Tradition of Jewish
Meditation By Avram Davis 4½ x 8, 176 pp, Quality PB, ISBN 1-58023-060-1 **$15.95**

Ritual/Sacred Practice/Journaling

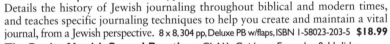

The Jewish Dream Book: The Key to Opening the Inner Meaning of
Your Dreams By Vanessa L. Ochs with Elizabeth Ochs; Full-color illus. by Kristina Swarner
Instructions for how modern people can perform ancient Jewish dream practices
and dream interpretations drawn from the Jewish wisdom tradition. For anyone
who wants to understand their dreams—and themselves.
8 x 8, 120 pp, Full-color illus., Deluxe PB w/flaps, ISBN 1-58023-132-2 **$16.95**

The Jewish Journaling Book: How to Use Jewish Tradition to Write
Your Life & Explore Your Soul By Janet Ruth Falon
Details the history of Jewish journaling throughout biblical and modern times,
and teaches specific journaling techniques to help you create and maintain a vital
journal, from a Jewish perspective. 8 x 8, 304 pp, Deluxe PB w/flaps, ISBN 1-58023-203-5 **$18.99**

The Book of Jewish Sacred Practices: CLAL's Guide to Everyday & Holiday
Rituals & Blessings Edited by Rabbi Irwin Kula and Vanessa L. Ochs, Ph.D.
6 x 9, 368 pp, Quality PB, ISBN 1-58023-152-7 **$18.95**

Jewish Ritual: A Brief Introduction for Christians
By Rabbi Kerry M. Olitzky and Rabbi Daniel Judson
5½ x 8½, 144 pp, Quality PB, ISBN 1-58023-210-8 **$14.99**

The Rituals & Practices of a Jewish Life: A Handbook for Personal Spiritual
Renewal Edited by Rabbi Kerry M. Olitzky and Rabbi Daniel Judson
6 x 9, 272 pp, illus., Quality PB, ISBN 1-58023-169-1 **$18.95**

Science Fiction/
Mystery & Detective Fiction

Mystery Midrash: An Anthology of Jewish Mystery & Detective Fiction
Edited by Lawrence W. Raphael. Preface by Joel Siegel.
6 x 9, 304 pp, Quality PB, ISBN 1-58023-055-5 **$16.95**

Criminal Kabbalah: An Intriguing Anthology of Jewish Mystery & Detective Fiction
Edited by Lawrence W. Raphael. Foreword by Laurie R. King.
6 x 9, 256 pp, Quality PB, ISBN 1-58023-109-8 **$16.95**

More Wandering Stars: An Anthology of Outstanding Stories of Jewish Fantasy and
Science Fiction Edited by Jack Dann. Introduction by Isaac Asimov.
6 x 9, 192 pp, Quality PB, ISBN 1-58023-063-6 **$16.95**

Wandering Stars: An Anthology of Jewish Fantasy & Science Fiction
Edited by Jack Dann. Introduction by Isaac Asimov.
6 x 9, 272 pp, Quality PB, ISBN 1-58023-005-9 **$16.95**

Spirituality/Women's Interest

The Quotable Jewish Woman: Wisdom, Inspiration & Humor from the Mind & Heart *Edited and compiled by Elaine Bernstein Partnow*
The definitive collection of ideas, reflections, humor, and wit of over 300 Jewish women.
6 x 9, 496 pp, Hardcover, ISBN 1-58023-193-4 **$29.99**

Lifecycles, Vol. 1: Jewish Women on Life Passages & Personal Milestones
Edited and with introductions by Rabbi Debra Orenstein 6 x 9, 480 pp, Quality PB, ISBN 1-58023-018-0 **$19.95**

Lifecycles, Vol. 2: Jewish Women on Biblical Themes in Contemporary Life
Edited and with introductions by Rabbi Debra Orenstein and Rabbi Jane Rachel Litman
6 x 9, 464 pp, Quality PB, ISBN 1-58023-019-9 **$19.95**

Moonbeams: A Hadassah Rosh Hodesh Guide *Edited by Carol Diament, Ph.D.*
8½ x 11, 240 pp, Quality PB, ISBN 1-58023-099-7 **$20.00**

ReVisions: Seeing Torah through a Feminist Lens *By Rabbi Elyse Goldstein*
5½ x 8½, 224 pp, Quality PB, ISBN 1-58023-117-9 **$16.95**

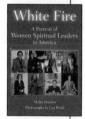

White Fire: A Portrait of Women Spiritual Leaders in America
By Rabbi Malka Drucker. Photographs by Gay Block.
7 x 10, 320 pp, 30+ b/w photos, Hardcover, ISBN 1-893361-64-0 **$24.95** *(A SkyLight Paths book)*

Women of the Wall: Claiming Sacred Ground at Judaism's Holy Site
Edited by Phyllis Chesler and Rivka Haut 6 x 9, 496 pp, b/w photos, Hardcover, ISBN 1-58023-161-6 **$34.95**

The Women's Haftarah Commentary: New Insights from Women Rabbis on the 54 Weekly Haftarah Portions, the 5 Megillot & Special Shabbatot
Edited by Rabbi Elyse Goldstein 6 x 9, 560 pp, Hardcover, ISBN 1-58023-133-0 **$39.99**

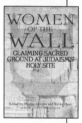

The Women's Torah Commentary: New Insights from Women Rabbis on the 54 Weekly Torah Portions *Edited by Rabbi Elyse Goldstein*
6 x 9, 496 pp, Hardcover, ISBN 1-58023-076-8 **$34.95**

The Year Mom Got Religion: One Woman's Midlife Journey into Judaism
By Lee Meyerhoff Hendler 6 x 9, 208 pp, Quality PB, ISBN 1-58023-070-9 **$15.95**

See Holidays for *The Women's Passover Companion: Women's Reflections on the Festival of Freedom* and *The Women's Seder Sourcebook: Rituals & Readings for Use at the Passover Seder.* Also see Bar/Bat Mitzvah for *The JGirl's Guide: The Young Jewish Woman's Handbook for Coming of Age.*

Travel

Israel—A Spiritual Travel Guide, 2nd Edition
A Companion for the Modern Jewish Pilgrim
By Rabbi Lawrence A. Hoffman 4¾ x 10, 256 pp, Quality PB, illus., ISBN 1-58023-261-2 **$18.99**
Also Available: **The Israel Mission Leader's Guide** ISBN 1-58023-085-7 **$4.95**

12 Steps

100 Blessings Every Day Daily Twelve Step Recovery Affirmations, Exercises for Personal Growth & Renewal Reflecting Seasons of the Jewish Year
By Rabbi Kerry M. Olitzky. Foreword by Rabbi Neil Gillman.
One-day-at-a-time monthly format. Reflects on the rhythm of the Jewish calendar to bring insight to recovery from addictions.
4½ x 6½, 432 pp, Quality PB, ISBN 1-879045-30-3 **$15.99**

Recovery from Codependence: A Jewish Twelve Steps Guide to Healing Your Soul
By Rabbi Kerry M. Olitzky 6 x 9, 160 pp, Quality PB, ISBN 1-879045-32-X **$13.95**

Renewed Each Day: Daily Twelve Step Recovery Meditations Based on the Bible
By Rabbi Kerry M. Olitzky and Aaron Z.
Vol. 1—Genesis & Exodus: 6 x 9, 224 pp, Quality PB, ISBN 1-879045-12-5 **$14.95**
Vol. 2—Leviticus, Numbers & Deuteronomy: 6 x 9, 280 pp, Quality PB, ISBN 1-879045-13-3 **$14.95**

Twelve Jewish Steps to Recovery: A Personal Guide to Turning from Alcoholism & Other Addictions—Drugs, Food, Gambling, Sex...
By Rabbi Kerry M. Olitzky and Stuart A. Copans, M.D. Preface by Abraham J. Twerski, M.D.
6 x 9, 144 pp, Quality PB, ISBN 1-879045-09-5 **$14.95**

Abraham Joshua Heschel

The Earth Is the Lord's: The Inner World of the Jew in Eastern Europe
5½ x 8, 128 pp, Quality PB, ISBN 1-879045-42-7 **$14.95**

Israel: An Echo of Eternity New Introduction by Susannah Heschel
5½ x 8, 272 pp, Quality PB, ISBN 1-879045-70-2 **$19.95**

A Passion for Truth: Despair and Hope in Hasidism
5½ x 8, 352 pp, Quality PB, ISBN 1-879045-41-9 **$18.99**

Holidays/Holy Days

Leading the Passover Journey
The Seder's Meaning Revealed, the Haggadah's Story Retold
By Rabbi Nathan Laufer
Uncovers the hidden meaning of the Seder's rituals and customs
6 x 9, 208 pp, Hardcover, ISBN 1-58023-211-6 **$24.99**

Reclaiming Judaism as a Spiritual Practice: Holy Days and Shabbat
By Rabbi Goldie Milgram

Provides a framework for understanding the powerful and often unexplained intellectual, emotional, and spiritual tools that are essential for a lively, relevant, and fulfilling Jewish spiritual practice. 7 x 9, 272 pp, Quality PB, ISBN 1-58023-205-1 **$19.99**

7th Heaven: Celebrating Shabbat with Rebbe Nachman of Breslov
By Moshe Mykoff with the Breslov Research Institute
Explores the art of consciously observing Shabbat and understanding in-depth many of the day's spiritual practices. 5⅛ x 8¼, 224 pp, Deluxe PB w/flaps, ISBN 1-58023-175-6 **$18.95**

The Women's Passover Companion
Women's Reflections on the Festival of Freedom
Edited by Rabbi Sharon Cohen Anisfeld, Tara Mohr, and Catherine Spector
Groundbreaking. A provocative conversation about women's relationships to Passover as well as the roots and meanings of women's seders.
6 x 9, 352 pp, Hardcover, ISBN 1-58023-128-4 **$24.95**

The Women's Seder Sourcebook
Rituals & Readings for Use at the Passover Seder
Edited by Rabbi Sharon Cohen Anisfeld, Tara Mohr, and Catherine Spector
Gathers the voices of more than one hundred women in readings, personal and creative reflections, commentaries, blessings, and ritual suggestions that can be incorporated into your Passover celebration.
6 x 9, 384 pp, Hardcover, ISBN 1-58023-136-5 **$24.95**

Creating Lively Passover Seders: A Sourcebook of Engaging Tales, Texts & Activities
By David Arnow, Ph.D. 7 x 9, 416 pp, Quality PB, ISBN 1-58023-184-5 **$24.99**

Hanukkah, 2nd Edition: The Family Guide to Spiritual Celebration
By Dr. Ron Wolfson. Edited by Joel Lurie Grishaver.
7 x 9, 240 pp, illus., Quality PB, ISBN 1-58023-122-5 **$18.95**

The Jewish Family Fun Book: Holiday Projects, Everyday Activities, and Travel Ideas with Jewish Themes *By Danielle Dardashti and Roni Sarig. Illus. by Avi Katz.*
6 x 9, 288 pp, 70+ b/w illus. & diagrams, Quality PB, ISBN 1-58023-171-3 **$18.95**

The Jewish Gardening Cookbook: Growing Plants & Cooking for
Holidays & Festivals *By Michael Brown* 6 x 9, 224 pp, 30+ illus., Quality PB, ISBN 1-58023-116-0 **$16.95**

The Jewish Lights Book of Fun Classroom Activities: Simple and Seasonal
Projects for Teachers and Students *By Danielle Dardashti and Roni Sarig*
6 x 9, 240 pp, Quality PB, ISBN 1-58023-206-X **$19.99**

Passover, 2nd Edition: The Family Guide to Spiritual Celebration
By Dr. Ron Wolfson with Joel Lurie Grishaver 7 x 9, 352 pp, Quality PB, ISBN 1-58023-174-8 **$19.95**

Shabbat, 2nd Edition: The Family Guide to Preparing for and Celebrating the Sabbath
By Dr. Ron Wolfson 7 x 9, 320 pp, illus., Quality PB, ISBN 1-58023-164-0 **$19.95**

Sharing Blessings: Children's Stories for Exploring the Spirit of the Jewish Holidays
By Rahel Musleah and Michael Klayman
8½ x 11, 64 pp, Full-color illus., Hardcover, ISBN 1-879045-71-0 **$18.95** *For ages 6 & up*

Life Cycle
Marriage / Parenting / Family / Aging

Jewish Fathers: A Legacy of Love
Photographs by Lloyd Wolf. Essays by Paula Wolfson. Foreword by Harold S. Kushner.
Honors the role of contemporary Jewish fathers in America. Each father tells in his own words what it means to be a parent and Jewish, and what he learned from his own father. Insightful photos. 9½ x 9⅞, 144 pp with 100+ duotone photos, Hardcover, ISBN 1-58023-204-3 **$30.00**

The New Jewish Baby Album: Creating and Celebrating the Beginning of a Spiritual Life—A Jewish Lights Companion
By the Editors at Jewish Lights. Foreword by Anita Diamant. Preface by Sandy Eisenberg Sasso.
A spiritual keepsake that will be treasured for generations. More than just a memory book, *shows you how—and why it's important*—to create a Jewish home and a Jewish life. 8 x 10, 64 pp, Deluxe Padded Hardcover, Full-color illus., ISBN 1-58023-138-1 **$19.95**

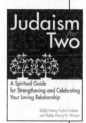

The Jewish Pregnancy Book: A Resource for the Soul, Body & Mind during Pregnancy, Birth & the First Three Months
By Sandy Falk, M.D., and Rabbi Daniel Judson, with Steven A. Rapp
Includes medical information, prayers and rituals for each stage of pregnancy, from a liberal Jewish perspective. 7 x 10, 208 pp, Quality PB, b/w illus., ISBN 1-58023-178-0 **$16.95**

Celebrating Your New Jewish Daughter: Creating Jewish Ways to Welcome Baby Girls into the Covenant—New and Traditional Ceremonies
By Debra Nussbaum Cohen 6 x 9, 272 pp, Quality PB, ISBN 1-58023-090-3 **$18.95**

The New Jewish Baby Book, 2nd Edition: Names, Ceremonies & Customs—A Guide for Today's Families *By Anita Diamant* 6 x 9, 336 pp, Quality PB, ISBN 1-58023-251-5 **$19.99**

Parenting As a Spiritual Journey: Deepening Ordinary and Extraordinary Events into Sacred Occasions *By Rabbi Nancy Fuchs-Kreimer* 6 x 9, 224 pp, Quality PB, ISBN 1-58023-016-4 **$16.95**

Judaism for Two: A Spiritual Guide for Strengthening and Celebrating Your Loving Relationship *By Rabbi Nancy Fuchs-Kreimer and Rabbi Nancy H. Wiener*
Addresses the ways Jewish teachings can enhance and strengthen committed relationships. 6 x 9, 208 pp, Quality PB, ISBN 1-58023-254-X **$16.99**

Embracing the Covenant: Converts to Judaism Talk About Why & How
By Rabbi Allan Berkowitz and Patti Moskovitz 6 x 9, 192 pp, Quality PB, ISBN 1-879045-50-8 **$16.95**

The Guide to Jewish Interfaith Family Life: An InterfaithFamily.com Handbook
Edited by Ronnie Friedland and Edmund Case 6 x 9, 384 pp, Quality PB, ISBN 1-58023-153-5 **$18.95**

Introducing My Faith and My Community
The Jewish Outreach Institute Guide for the Christian in a Jewish Interfaith Relationship
By Rabbi Kerry M. Olitzky 6 x 9, 176 pp, Quality PB, ISBN 1-58023-192-6 **$16.99**

Making a Successful Jewish Interfaith Marriage: The Jewish Outreach Institute Guide to Opportunities, Challenges and Resources
By Rabbi Kerry M. Olitzky with Joan Peterson Littman 6 x 9, 176 pp, Quality PB, ISBN 1-58023-170-5 **$16.95**

The Creative Jewish Wedding Book: A Hands-On Guide to New & Old Traditions, Ceremonies & Celebrations *By Gabrielle Kaplan-Mayer*
Provides the tools to create the most meaningful Jewish traditional or alternative wedding by using ritual elements to express your unique style and spirituality. 9 x 9, 288 pp, b/w photos, Quality PB, ISBN 1-58023-194-2 **$19.99**

Divorce Is a Mitzvah: A Practical Guide to Finding Wholeness and Holiness When Your Marriage Dies *By Rabbi Perry Netter. Afterword by Rabbi Laura Geller.*
6 x 9, 224 pp, Quality PB, ISBN 1-58023-172-1 **$16.95**

A Heart of Wisdom: Making the Jewish Journey from Midlife through the Elder Years
Edited by Susan Berrin. Foreword by Harold Kushner. 6 x 9, 384 pp, Quality PB, ISBN 1-58023-051-2 **$18.95**

So That Your Values Live On: Ethical Wills and How to Prepare Them
Edited by Jack Riemer and Nathaniel Stampfer 6 x 9, 272 pp, Quality PB, ISBN 1-879045-34-6 **$18.95**